THE SCIMITAR
AND ITS FOREBEARS

by
DON PITHER

— COURT PUBLISHING —

©Copyright 1987 — Don Pither Esq.

ISBN 0 9512873 0 3.

All Rights Reserved. No part of this publication may be reproduced, stored in a retrieval system or transmitted in any form or by any means, electronic, mechanical, photocopying, recording or otherwise, without prior permission of Court Publishing.

First published — October 1987.

Published by Court Publishing, Droys Court, Witcombe, Gloucester GL3 4TN.

Text set in 10 on 12pt Palatino.
Printed and bound by Manor Park Press Ltd,
Edison Road, Eastbourne, East Sussex BN23 6PT.

Front cover:
The author's faithful SE5a at Paris House, Woburn.

Back cover:
The newly announced 2.8 litre GTE & GTC on a North Wales beach.

Tom Williams, founder of Reliant Motor Co.

To
Margaret

Contents

Foreword		vii
Introduction		ix
Chapter 1	Three-wheeled origins	1
Chapter 2	The Sabre	21
Chapter 3	Sabres in rallying	41
Chapter 4	The Ogle connection	69
Chapter 5	Grand Touring Estate	95
Chapter 6	The Scimitar matures	129
Chapter 7	Drophead alternative	149
Chapter 8	A new young blade	163
Chapter 9	What might have been	179
Chapter 10	Owner's guide	193
Appendix		201
Index		227

HRH The Princess Royal with her first GTE.

BUCKINGHAM PALACE

      Before I started my driving career, my father had an interesting car to drive. It had a new Ogle design GTE fibre glass body and a lot of glass. I didn't see much of it but it struck me as a very practical but sporty little car.

      Time moved on and I passed my driving test and after much discussion it was decided that I could have a Rover 2000 TC and I was very pleased with it. However, about three years later I came across a Reliant Scimitar GTE which I was allowed to drive. Four months later I was the proud owner of my first Scimitar and now sixteen years later I'm driving my eighth - I think! I have enjoyed sixteen years of relatively trouble free driving and have consistently surprised other people with its performance and load carrying capacity. It will be very difficult to find a replacement for it should the worst happen and the Scimitar is no longer manufactured. I have also used the Reliant Regal and Robin.

      I'm delighted that Mr. Pither has taken the time and effort to put this book together which I am sure will give a lot of pleasure to past and present Reliant owners. I think we are a friendly bunch who still enjoy motoring rather than having a car simply as a means of transport. I very much hope we shall be able to continue to enjoy our motoring, but if not we shall now have an important souvenir of a unique car.

Anne

Photo Credits

Source	Page(s)
'Autocar'	3, 4, 20, 19 (top), 21, 36, 78, 79, 80, 81, 168, 176
'Autosport'	33, 44, 105
Peter Bailey	101, 104, 110
Tony Breckell	162 (top)
'Classic & Sportscar'	27, 63
'Clickstops'	68
Foster & Skeffington	66
Pete Hackett	89
John Hopwood	45
Bernard Jackson	15, 112, 114
LAT	1, 6, 38, 41, 46, 48, 49 (top), 50, 59 (bottom), 140, 141, 147
Ogle Design	72, 73, 74, 75, 76, 77, 98, 111 (bottom), 180, 181, 182, 189
J. Devlin	196
Andrew Moreland	163, 171, XV (bottom)
'Motor'	24, 52, 53, 153
Reg Mottram	17, 19 (bottom), 131
National Motor Museum	13, 32, 82, 86
Don Pither	92, 94, 97, 102, 103, 108, 118, 129, 134, 144, 145, 146, 149, 155, 174, 175, 184, 185, 191, 192, 197, 198, 225, XIII (bottom), front cover, XIV (bottom)
Robin Rew	56, 64, 67, 193
Reliant Motor PLC	11, 12, 14, 15, 16, 18, 25, 26, 30, 34, 35, 40, 69, 83, 88, 90, 95, 99, 106, 107, 109, 111 (top), 113, 116, 117, 121, 122, 125, 127, 128, 132, 133, 135, 137, 139, 143, 148, 157, 159, 160, 161, 162 (bottom), 169, 170, 172, 173, 177, 188, XIV (top), rear cover, XV (top), XVI (top).
Mrs. A. Rusling (via Guy Smith)	8, 39, 47, 49 (bottom), 51, 55, 58, 60, 61, 65, XIII (top)
'Sports Car Monthly'	XVI (bottom)
D. Slaney	7, 9, 10, 31, 37, 91, 93
Tony Stevens	166, 167
Triplex Glass Co. Ltd	84, 85, 87
John Walker	115, 124, 126
Mrs. T. Williams	Frontispiece
Barrie Wills	179, 187
Ken Wood	152, 153, 154, 156, 183

Introduction

My first awareness of Reliant sports cars was their rallying activities in 1963-64 when, at the age of 24, I was in the habit of charging round the Welsh valleys in a Mini at the dead of night on club rallies. Rallying has always been the most attractive form of sport for me and the enterprising efforts of the relatively uncompetitive Sabres seemed so admirable at the time. We even had a Sabre agent in my home town of Gloucester, at Three Cocks Motors near the Cathedral, where I first set eyes upon the anglicised Israeli car. My interest has frequently been aroused by the unusual aspects of life and machinery, for which the Sabre qualifies unquestionably, along with the Daimler Dart and the Ogle designs applied to both. The resulting Scimitar Coupé came as close to my ideal car as anything available in the mid 1960s, having the potential of economical high performance combined with longevity and flair. One possible improvement might have been the adoption of the Daimler V8 engine mounted in the superior Reliant chassis. That basic formula still makes sense to this day and some owners have virtually achieved a parallel version by inserting the even nicer alloy Rover V8 engine, some 20 years after the car's inception.

I can still remember the shock of seeing a small news item in 1968, at the foot of a page of 'The Daily Telegraph', announcing the introduction of the Scimitar GTE. The profile illustrated immediately struck me as just right for an all-round GT car and resembled so closely the picture of a special estate version of the Fiat Dino, called the Ginerva, which adorned a wall in my flat. Having a degree in Chemistry and working on plastics with Shell Chemical Company, I found the skilful use of corrosion proof reinforced plastic bodywork for cars very logical and attractive. Another feature of the Reliant range which appealed to me very much was its separate chassis, and how I drooled over the bare rolling GTE chassis at the 1968 Motor Show! While I am not blind to the overwhelming advantages of a monocoque bodyshell for mass-producing cars and attaining high levels of rigidity combined with low weight, my own preference is for a galvanised steel base frame clothed in rot-free bodywork. This combination featured in the latter years of the GTE production as it does in a more sophisticated form in another of my ideal cars, the Renault Espace.

It was not until 1976 that I was actually able to own a GTE, a one owner 1974 model, so that I could test my firmly held beliefs. I was not to be disappointed and I still own the same car to this day, albeit now Rover V8 powered, but original in all structural aspects. Little did I realise the significance of the purchase of that April Yellow machine, which subsequently opened up a new field of motor sport — hill climbing — in the course of which I met my wife, started a new career as a Scimitar spares specialist and finally produced this book.

During the past ten years this faithful SE5a spent two hard seasons in competition before acting as a goods vehicle for my spares business, a tow car for the racing Sabre and more recently has taken me hundreds of miles in search of material for you to read in the pages that follow. Its retirement from competition in 1978 was not because of frailty, but due to the acquisition of another, even older, Reliant specifically for sprint and race events, in the shape of a Sabre Six (92 FRP), modified to the same standards as the rally Sabres in most respects. FRP, as she is affectionately known in Owners' Club circles, gave me more fun and success than any other car I have ever owned and still holds two class records, set in 1984, at Prescott and Gurston Down hill climbs.

Parting with FRP was necessary to pursue my latest Reliant competition project, in conjunction with Les Trafford. The 'Yellow Brick', as it has become known, is based on a standard SE5a chassis and body, suitably lightened, but powered by an enlarged Rover V8 engine supercharged by belt-drive blower. In only its second year in competitive hill climbing Les Trafford took it to victory in the Unlimited Racing Sports Car Class of the Midland Hill Climb Championship against Porsche, Morgan and AC. This must be the only occasion that a GTE in any form has won a competition championship of any sort.

While in my own mind the SE5a is the definitive Scimitar, one cannot deny the extra space and comfort provided by the SE6 series, and the decision by Reliant to extend the range by producing the convertible GTC was excellent. Quite why this superb car was so slow to sell is very difficult to determine, unless it was because of price. Nevertheless, there was nothing like it at anywhere near the £11,000 mark in 1981 and it was so much better than the discontinued Stag in so many ways, except possibly appearance, that it should have succeeded. Now it is destined to become a collector's item as only 442 examples were made.

I hope the foregoing illustrates my enthusiasm for the Scimitar in all its forms, but I trust that I have not been too blinkered by this not to have recognised and mentioned its deficiencies as well. I have tried in the following pages to give as complete and accurate account of the background to this significant range of British cars as was possible from what little archive material remains.

I could not have been more highly honoured than by the kind acceptance of HRH The Princess Royal to write the foreword to my book. Her own enthusiasm for the Scimitar is widely known and indeed her patronage of the model must have contributed enormously to its stature in the eyes of the general public as well as among enthusiasts. I am immensely grateful to Her Royal Highness and her staff for setting the seal on this book about one of Britain's better achievements.

Finally, my task has been assisted immeasurably by the following friends and contacts (particularly as I tragically missed the disposal of most of the Reliant archive material, which could have been so valuable in this project, by only a matter of months). Without their help I could not have hoped to piece together what is, I hope, a fairly complete picture of the development of the Scimitar and fill an obvious gap in the motoring literature in the same way that Reliant have tried to do with their cars in the UK market.

I would like to express here my eternal thanks to my long-suffering wife, Margaret, who typed every word of the manuscript; to my mother-in-law, Mrs. Kay Turner, who so patiently proof-read the galleys as well as painstakingly compiled the index and to Peter Longstaff-Tyrrell who offered his printing expertise voluntarily in the design and production of this book.

Don Pither

Witcombe, Gloucester
July 1987

ACKNOWLEDGEMENTS

Peter Bailey, Liz Baines, Nigel Baker, Mike Bennett, Tony Breckell, Peter Brock, John Crosthwaite, Mrs. Joe Devlin, Edward Eves, John Hopwood, Bernard Jackson, Tom Karen, Peter Longstaff-Tyrrell, Anne Moore, Andrew Moreland, Reg Mottram, Jon Pressnell, Mrs. Arthur Rusling, D. Slaney, Denis Smith, Guy Smith, Ritchie Spencer, Tony Stafford, Simon Taylor, Mrs. Kay Turner, John Walker, Ray Wiggin, Mrs. Tom Williams, Barrie Wills, Gerry Wilmott, Ken Wood.

Three-wheeled origins

THE POWER BENEATH THE RELIANT BONNET

Developed over the years into trouble-free unit, the Reliant four-cylinder water-cooled engine has more than ample power for its purpose, and it is fitted with our own four-speed and reverse synchromesh gearbox. Again, most of the components, including the crankshaft, camshaft and gears, are produced in our own factory. This also ensures the ready availability of spare parts when needed.

Reliant
MARK VI SALOON

This is the result of those years of steady development that has put Reliant so far ahead of all its competitors. It embodies all those features already described as well as a car-type rear axle and hydraulic brakes and dampers

REGAL BY NAME
REGAL IN PERFORMANCE

BODY
Pioneers in the use of fibreglass for motor bodies, we have combined modern styling with a tough construction plus freedom from rust. Another notable feature is its ease of repair.

CHASSIS
Box section, pressed steel with tubular crossmembers forming a very rigid and durable construction. Produced entirely in the Reliant Assembly Shop.

SEATS
Produced in our factory for lightness and comfort, the seats have a light alloy tubular frame, special resilient webbing, upholstered in the latest plastic foam and neatly trimmed in hard wearing leathercloth.

FACIA PANEL
A comprehensive range of immediately visible instruments are grouped centrally in the fibreglass panel. Two extra large easily accessible compartments are placed either side of the instruments.

EXPERIENCE THE JOY OF MOTORING IN A RELIANT!

Reliant ENGINEERING CO. (TAMWORTH) LTD

Watling Street, Twogates, Tamworth, Staffs.
Phone: Tamworth 336. Grams: RELIANT, TAMWORTH 336

CHAPTER 1

Three-wheeled origins

THE ORIGINS OF the Scimitar are inextricably linked with the development of the Reliant three- and four-wheeled economy cars. Even though there are no common design links, apart from the principle of a fibreglass body mounted on a steel chassis, it was the sales success of the small cars that allowed the company to indulge in the production of a range of sporting and very distinctive up-market motor cars.

The Reliant Motor Company must now rank as the third oldest British owned car producer and possibly the third largest after ARG and Jaguar with the demise of so many British marques during the last decade. The first prototype Reliant — a three-wheeled van — was licenced on 1st January 1935, which was the same year William Lyons floated his SS Cars as a public company. The founder of the Reliant Engineering Company was Tom Lawrence Williams, at the age of 44, having spent a career in engineering commencing with heavy steam vehicles before joining Triumph in 1916 where he designed its first chain driven motorcycle. In 1924 he moved to the Sheffield company Dunford and Elliott, to take charge of the new range of Dunelt motorcycles for six years before transferring to Raleigh in Nottingham. There he designed the Safety Seven three-wheeler powered by an air-cooled 742cc V-twin engine of which 3,000 were sold from 1933-1936. Such was his conviction in the future of three-wheelers in this country, Williams left Raleigh in 1934 to produce his own version of the Safety Seven from a workshop in the garden of his Tamworth home. The design was based on a live rear axle and a single front wheel suspended motorcycle fashion on sprung forks with handlebar control for steering. Tom Williams launched his new company with

1950 Regent 10cwt van using 747cc Austin engine

the help of loans of £500 each from his wife and sister, plus the timely maturity of a Sun Life of Canada Insurance policy. His first assistant, later to become an employee for 30 years, was 'Tommo' Thompson who retired less than a week before Tom himself died.

During the four years leading up to the outbreak of the Second World War, premises were found on the present Two Gates site previously used as a Midland Red bus garage. Here offices were built and as sales increased, plant was acquired for mass-production. This not only involved assembly of the small commercials, but also the production of their own 747cc side valve engine derived from the Austin 7 engine Reliant had been using originally. Like most motor manufacturers during the War, Reliant were diverted onto Government engineering contracts until hostilities ceased in 1945. Three-wheel vans were again produced in 1946 on the pre-war 8cwt design which was uprated to a 10cwt Regent model in 1950. The first landmark for this young company came in the Coronation year of 1953 with the introduction of their first passenger car. It had a coach-built aluminium body mounted on a new box-section chassis now using a steering wheel and steering box instead of handlebar and a rear-hinged leading arm locating the single front wheel sprung by a torsion bar inside the front cross tube. To save weight, the side and rear windows were made of Perspex, but they only afforded limited visibility. Performance from the 16bhp engine was modest to say the least with a maximum speed approaching 60mph, but owners could console themselves with an average fuel consumption of 45mpg. Perhaps due to the Royal significance of the Coronation year, the car was called the Regal, which was developed to the Mk III version by

1956 Regal MkIII, Britain's first quantity produced car with all GRP body.

1956. This model was fitted with a body made from glass-reinforced polyester resin (GRP or fibreglass as it is now known) still mounted on an ash framework. This really was a second landmark for Reliant since all subsequent vehicles produced by the company utilised this material for the bodywork.

The traditional hand lay-up procedure was used in the moulding process whereby polyester resin mixed with a catalyst hardener is first spread over the surface of the mould to form the finished gel-coat. Pre-cut sections of fibreglass matting are then laid on this uncured layer while more resin is worked into the matting before a second layer of fibreglass is added and treated in the same fashion. The resulting laminate is allowed to cure at normal temperatures, although Reliant later passed the moulds through heated tunnels to accelerate the curing process. Finally the hardened moulding is removed from the mould and excess material at the edges is trimmed off to attain the correct shape.

The unitary principle of construction was introduced in 1962 in which the inner and outer shells were first moulded, separately, then bonded together to form a fully integrated fibreglass bodyshell now mounted on a steel chassis.

This development coincided with the acquisition of a 76% controlling interest in the Reliant Motor Company by the Gwent based Hodge Group, whose founder, Sir Julian Hodge, became Chairman of the Reliant Motor Group now consisting of Reliant Motor Company, Hodgkinson Bennis, Press Operations (makers of chassis pressings for Reliant) and Smiths Forgings. Ray Wiggin became Managing Director of Reliant as well as a Board member of the other companies in the Group following the death of Tom Williams two years later.

Reliant's initiative into fibreglass bodywork seemed to spawn a new minor industry producing bodyshells of the same material for fitting to existing production car chassis giving rise to the era of specials and kit-cars. The introduction of VAT in 1973 curtailed many of these enterprises and only a handful have survived apart from Reliant, notably TVR, Lotus, Marcos and Ginetta. In the 1980s we are seeing a resurgence of this type of industry on an even larger scale mainly due to the rapid deterioration of the steel bodywork of cars produced in the 1970s yielding chassis and mechanical components capable of being dressed up in far more exciting fibreglass confections of widely differing quality. It remains to be seen how many of these entrepreneurial concerns withstand the pressure of time and competition from the few major manufacturers remaining. The market for such kit-cars and replicas in particular is no doubt fuelled by the narrower choice of designs, however good they may be, from the reduced numbers of marques producing 'world cars'.

One of the main reasons for Reliant's survival was the degree of self-sufficiency established from the very beginning with the production of their own engines and gearboxes in 1939. Reliant were also very clever in producing a range of vehicles not offered by their larger competitors, but for which there was nevertheless sufficient demand to match the production capacity of the company. In 1963 a new factory was opened by motor racing champion Jim Clark at Shenstone, some seven miles along the A5 from Two Gates, to house the manufacture of mechanical components. Eventually as much as 80% of the parts required for production were made there. Engine blocks, crankshafts, camshafts and gears were all machined in this new factory from their own designs and virtually the only components bought in consisted of brakes, electrical, glass and some trim and control accessories. About 300 employees produced around 400 new all alloy engines, gearboxes and axles per week at Shenstone.

Reliant-produced all alloy 600cc ohv engines.

Three-Wheeled Origins

Three-wheeler production line at Two Gates factory.

The new engines were now of 600cc capacity with ohv cylinder heads and first appeared in the Regal 3/25 car which featured the controversial reverse slope rear window pioneered by the Ford 105E Anglia. Reliant were then the first manufacturer to introduce an all alloy engine on a mass-production basis, ahead of the Hillman Imp, and the main reason for choosing such a material for engine construction was for light weight. In order to comply with the licensing regulations three-wheeled cars could only be taxed and licenced at motorcycle rates if their kerb weight was below 8cwt. It was this low running cost that made this range of cars so successful as they particularly appealed to ex-motorcyclists with families.

Following a fire in the body moulding shop at Two Gates, a new six acre factory was acquired in 1966 at Kettlebrook in Tamworth, specifically for fibreglass moulding. About 600 people were employed at the new site, mainly producing three-wheeler bodies on a continuous process. Racked lines of inner and outer body moulds were successively washed, dried, polished, gel-coated with resin, layed-up with matt and allowed to cure. The moulds were mounted in such a fashion that they could be rotated completely so that floor-pan, sides and roof could be moulded simultaneously. Some panels of limited size, such as doors and bonnets, were produced by hot pressing sheets of resin-impregnated fibreglass matting between metal dies. It was essential to keep a close scrutiny on the amount of materials used in the moulding process to avoid exceeding the stipulated maximum weight of the finished car.

This remarkable Regal 3/25 driven by Cyril 'Flash' Rogers survived a 5,211 mile proving run to the Sahara Desert and later completed the Monte Carlo Rally as a press car.

Three-Wheeled Origins

The chassis were welded up at Two Gates and transported to Kettlebrook to be mated with the cured bodyshells. The combined unit was mounted on a trolley where it remained for its journey back to Two Gates and through the assembly line there until the road wheels were fitted.

By the late 1960s, the capacity of the new engine had been increased to 700cc, so that the uprated Regal 3/30 could maintain its dominance of the three-wheeler market against its only competitor, the Bond 875, made in Preston. Reliant resolved that situation finally in 1969 by taking over Bond Cars even though the latter were only producing 1,500 cars a year, as opposed to Reliant's annual output of 15,000 three-wheelers. Since both the Regal and the Bond were fighting for the same market it should be no surprise that the Bond, with its expensive Hillman Imp engine and lower sales, had to be sacrificed. What really attracted Wiggin about Bond was their four-wheeled 2-litre Equipe models based on the Triumph Vitesse running gear. These quite elegant fibreglass bodied GT cars slotted nicely into the existing Reliant range of cars between the Regal and the newly introduced Scimitar as well as allowing the company access to Triumph dealer outlets.

Far from abandoning the Bond name, Wiggin commissioned their design consultants, Ogle, to produce a three-wheeler leisure vehicle to become known as the Bond Bug. The Bug used the Regal

The Ogle-bodied Bond Bug.

mechanicals apart from the coil spring over telescopic damper rear suspension in place of leaf springs to allow the bodywork to terminate immediately behind the rear axle. This outlandish vehicle, only available in obligatory orange paintwork, featured a lift-up front canopy incorporating the windscreen to gain access to the front seats. The Bug was one of the favourite designs of Tom Karen, the head of Ogle Design, who strove to create a practical car for the young motorist which would put the fun back into motoring. Reliant responded by offering a 'package for youth' finance scheme for those who could not afford the outright price which ranged from £548 for a Bare Bug to £628 for the Super version. Sadly it was not taken very seriously by the young motorists as had been hoped despite its use by such comedians as Jimmy Tarbuck and Bob Monkhouse. An extraordinary 'Double Bug' appeared on the Bond stand of the 1970 Motor Show where visitors were told that they could only buy 'half the car on show'.

A disected Bug at the Motor Show.

Three-Wheeled Origins

Reliant 750 Formula National Championship Trophy.

Testing flexibility of Reliant Robin bodywork!

By 1975 the Bug had been exterminated and the Bond name disappeared with it too as the Equipe saloon and convertible had ceased production by that time, even though Reliant had developed a replacement bodyshell in their own Development Department which never saw the light of day. It is difficult to see in retrospect exactly what Reliant gained by the acquisition of Bond Cars apart from eliminating their only competition in the three-wheeler division of which they were already obvious leaders. The reign of the Regal had come to an end by 1973 when it received a completely new body emanating from Ogle design incorporating an opening rear window to gain access to the luggage area as on the earlier Hillman Imp and erstwhile forebear Bond 875. The smooth newcomer, amusingly christened the Robin, was now powered by a 750cc version of the Reliant produced alloy engine yielding 32bhp at 5,500rpm. This engine now attracted the junior racing fraternity, namely the 750 Motor Club whose formula was based on the original Austin 7 engine. With the demise of that particular unit, what better engine could they adopt than its logical successor, now being produced in such large quantities at Tamworth? Thus the Robin engine became standard issue for all 750cc single seaters in ever more powerful form and has even been modified for use in motor boats and portable fire pumps as a result of its light weight and economy.

A surprising compliment was paid to the Robin when HRH The Princess Anne acquired a Super saloon when she was living at the Sandhurst Royal Academy. The final expansion of the engine capacity to 850cc in 1976 endowed the Robin with a respectable maximum speed of 80mph and 0-60mph time of 16.1 sec. Naturally economy was a big attraction, but the overall test figure of 40mpg is now exceeded in the late 1980s by cars of far higher performance. After eight years in production the Robin was succeeded by the wedge-shaped Rialto in 1981 offered at a price ranging from £2,900 to £3,700 when a Mini 1000 could be bought for £3,031 and a Citroen 2CV for only £2,300. Such a price handicap has not prevented the Rialto still being in high demand, much to the surprise of its makers who suffer recurrent fears that their perennial three-wheeler bread-winner will eventually fall out of favour. It must be said that Reliant had made great efforts to improve the interior fittings of the Rialto as well as galvanising the chassis. These factors allied to the legendary low running costs no doubt explain its continued popularity.

Latest three-wheeler — wedge shaped Rialto in estate form.

Three-Wheeled Origins

13

Despite the dominance of the three-wheeler theme, with which Reliant will always be associated, the company did divert into four-wheeled vehicle production way back in 1958, when they designed and developed a station wagon — estate car in today's parlance — for Autocars Limited of Haifa in Israel. This coincided with the recruitment of Ray Wiggin as assistant General Manager at the age of 29. Wiggin was intensely interested in Israel and its people and it was his influence which led to the contract between Reliant and Autocars to join forces in the production of a utility car. Assembly of the new vehicle, called the Sussita, took place in Israel using kits exported from Tamworth. Bodyshells were moulded locally from moulds supplied by Reliant who also provided expertise in setting up production. Neither this car nor its saloon counterpart the Carmel, also developed by Reliant, ever reached the British market. It was not

Autocar's Carmel designed and engineered by Reliant for production in Israel.

until 1964, the year in which the company founder Tom Williams died, that Reliant offered a four-wheeled car in the UK in the form of the 600cc Rebel saloon and estate, both shaped by Ogle. Ray Wiggin was now made Managing Director and felt, along with many of his staff, that the demand for the three-wheelers must soon diminish with rising standards of living, thus the introduction of a more competitive and conventional car seemed necessary. The construction of the Rebel was similar to the contemporary three-wheelers with the addition of double wishbone and coil spring independent front suspension mostly produced in house. However apt the name Rebel may have been, it never achieved the sales success hoped for due to its price of £525 compared with its mass-produced competitors such as the Mini (£470), Anglia (£479), Imp (£509) and Fiat 600 (£470). Even though its engine size was increased during its production life to 750cc, it was still down on power, hence performance, compared with its rivals, with only durability and fuel economy in its favour. Reliant repeated the exercise in 1976 when they introduced a four-wheeled counterpart to the Robin called the Kitten which also appeared in estate form like the Rebel and Robin models. The Kitten was still uncompetitive on price being £198 more than a Mini and £144 dearer than a Ford Escort.

The Rebel was the first four-wheeled economy car marketed by Reliant in the UK.

Three-Wheeled Origins

The more stylish Kitten succeeded the Rebel having a similar chassis as shown here, but neither was a commercial success.

However, Reliant were hoping to retain loyal three-wheeler customers who, for family reasons, had to graduate to a larger vehicle. The estate version even received the approval from the outspoken Editor of 'Motor Sport' who used one for many years. At least the fuel economy was outstanding as demonstrated by an RAC observed run when 75.30mpg was achieved on a country route averaging 30mph and perhaps even more impressive 71.0mpg while driving through London. This was emphasised by an outright win of the Mobil Economy Run at 55.11mpg. The three-wheeler Robin was still the favourite and production figures in 1976 were in the ratio of 250 Robins per week to only 80 Kittens. The introduction of the Kitten coincided with a rather bad patch for Reliant as a recall on the Robin to correct weak steering box mountings had cost the company £½ million, some of which had to be borrowed.

The Kitten estate was very practical and economic and well respected in many motoring circles.

Three-Wheeled Origins

Fortunately the export business was expanding following the initial co-operative venture with Autocars in Israel to produce kits for their Sussita and Carmel (FW3 model in Reliant terms) Ray Wiggin paid many visits to the Middle East during his early years in office and gained additional contracts, first in Turkey then later in Greece and India. With the aid of Ogle Design, the Reliant Bodywork and Engineering Departments under Ken Wood and David Page produced moulds and chassis of a two door saloon and estate car known as the Anadol (FW5) for the Otosan Company in Istanbul. Although quite conventional in concept with coil and wishbone front suspension and leaf sprung rear axle and powered by a Ford 1,200cc or 1,500cc Cortina engine and gearbox. The first prototype was driven overland to Turkey in 1966 and soon afterwards assembly started at the Otosan factory under the initial supervision of Reliant experts.

Anadols coming off the assembly line of the Otosan factory in Istanbul.

Initially production was at a rate of 600 cars per year, of which Reliant exported 85% of the content level. Progressively the Turks produced more components locally so that after ten years Reliant were supplying only 15% of the Anadol, but as production was now at a rate of 12,000 cars per year it was still very satisfactory business. In 1979 a five door prototype (FW11) was sent to Turkey for evaluation. Ray Wiggin had now been replaced as Managing Director by Ritchie Spencer whose new thinking employed Bertone to design the bodywork, which closely resembled the contemporary VW Passat and Chrysler Alpine. The chassis design was again very conventional and adaptable for Ford engines from 1.3-litre to 2.8-litre V6. The new car never reached production stage for economic reasons.

Reliant were also able to capitalise on their obsolete home products by selling the design rights abroad, as they did when the Kitten was finally withdrawn from the UK market in 1982. Sunrise Auto Industries (SAIL) of Bangalore in India purchased the moulds for this model and combined with engines exported from Reliant produced it locally and sold it under the name Dolphin. A light commercial version of the Kitten, the Fox, was developed for Greece in knocked-down form and has now appeared in the UK market as a Reliant model alongside the Rialto.

The stillborn Bertone-designed FW11 prototype intended to replace the Anadol.

Three-Wheeled Origins

The Fox pick-up derived from the Kitten was first produced in Greece before coming on to the UK market in 1984.

This Anadol was the outright winner of the gruelling 570 mile Trace Rally in Turkey.

Significantly, the Israeli firm of Autocars, who first commissioned Reliant to build a four wheeled car, were also the instigators who drew the Tamworth firm into the realm of more sporting machinery. The Managing Director of Autocars at the time of the Sussita project, Mr. Shubinsky, who was clearly well pleased with the joint operation so far, decided that in order for them to expand into exports to the USA they needed a two seater sports model, following the success of the MG and Triumph in that continent. During a visit to the 1960 Sports and Racing Car Show in London, Shubinsky was attracted by the Ashley bodyshell being exhibited there for fitting to Austin 7 or Ford 8 chassis. The material used for the bodies was fibreglass so suited their existing production facilities, but the chassis option was hardly suitable for the export field. Coincidentally at the same show Les Ballamy was displaying one of his chassis designed for a model known as the EB Debonair. This used Ford engines and running gear including the transverse leaf springs for the front and rear suspensions, but employing Ballamy's own means of wheel location. The combination appealed to the Israeli executive who immediately suggested to Reliant that the use of these ready made designs would be an ideal basis for their own sports car. Both sides agreed this was a feasible operation following which Autocars went ahead and acquired the rights to use the Ashley body design and Ballamy's chassis. As part of the deal the body moulds were included, as were a quantity of ready made chassis components and pressings from Ballamy, so presumably both vendors curtailed trading in those particular lines at that point. Thus Reliant were presented with the task of marrying the two concepts to produce a compatible entity to be known as the Sabra, after a species of Cactus peculiar to Israel.

Les Ballamy's chassis for the EB Debonair kit car.

The Ashley GT bodyshell marketed to fit Austin 7 or Ford 8 chassis.

The Sabre

piloting
the new
Sabre
sports
is a
startling*
experience

* STARTLING because here is a big sports car with a sparkling performance, but with a renowned power unit of 1700 c.c., 13′ 9″ overall length, 4′ 2″ high, 5′ 1″ wide and a weight of only 15¾ cwt.

* STARTLING because here is open car motoring with luxury saloon car comfort. Wind-up windows, wide opening doors, high quality interior appointments (wood-rimmed wheel, full instrumentation, luxury carpeting).

* STARTLING performance up to 100 m.p.h in standard form with powerful front disc brakes for safe stopping.

* STARTLING because in the Sabre all normal extras are fitted as standard, heater, complete range of instruments, windscreen washers, electric clock, wood-rimmed wheel, twin horns, self-parking wipers, cigar lighter.

* STARTLING because the superbly finished fibreglass body (mounted on a solid full-box section chassis) represents the latest in aerodynamic techniques.

* STARTLING because the Sabre opens up a new field of big, luxury sports car motoring

Reliant *Sabre* Swept Motoring

a new sports car experience

The SABRE is at the Motor Show Stand No. 146.

Engineered by THE RELIANT ENGINEERING CO. (TAMWORTH) LTD.

CHAPTER 2

The Sabre

THE 'SABRA' PROJECT was entrusted by a largely uninterested Tom Williams to Ray Wiggin, who had by now made a meteoric rise to Deputy Managing Director, under the direct control of Colin Thompson. Wiggin chose David Page to work on the chassis and running gear while Ken Wood specialised on the bodywork and fittings. It cannot have been an enviable task trying to co-ordinate two different designers work to produce a viable product capable of being mass-produced with little in the way of a free hand when choosing certain vital components. Firstly, Les Ballamy's chassis of the ladder type was fairly sound, but the choice of front suspension design was very curious indeed. It comprised a large tubular semi-swing axle pivoted at $38\frac{1}{2}°$ to the longitudinal of the car to form a compromise between a normal divided axle and a true leading link as on the Citroen 2CV. A transverse leaf spring of Ford derivation was attached to the outer end of each link to act as the suspension medium. Even on paper it was clear that the respective arcs of movement of the suspension arm and the leaf spring were totally in conflict and when a prototype was built using this configuration the spring promptly and not unexpectedly sheared at the ends. This happened even before the prototype (which is now being restored incidentally by Keith Healey of Walsall) had reached the factory gates. The simplest solution to this problem was soon devised by David Page, whereby the Ford-derived leaf spring was discarded in favour of two coil

The Les Ballamy chassis adopted by Autocars as the basis for their Sabra featuring the unconventional leading-link front suspension with leaf spring.

spring/damper units anchored to two vertical extensions on the front of the chassis. In order to provide front disc brakes, front hub, king pin and disc assemblies from the Standard Vanguard were grafted on to the leading links in place of the Ford parts intended. David was none too keen on the transverse leaf suspension at the rear either since here it was also required to provide lateral location of the rear axle via shackles at either end — good enough for a Ford Popular maybe, but hardly suitable for a sports car. Again coil springs over dampers were substituted for the leaf spring and a rather cunning if controversial method was used to provide axle location. Originally Ballamy used two trailing links splayed out from the chassis at some 15°, which were excellent for providing fore and aft location, but without the leaf spring no traverse location was present. One of the briefs for the whole design was that the original chassis members and suspension links had to be employed for the simple reason that so much of this hardware had already been purchased as part of the deal agreed by Autocars in the first place. David Page devised a very economic solution by simply moving the top trailing link on each side through 180° and fixing one end to the now raised rear portion of the chassis necessitated by using coil springs as at the front. Fore and aft location was still maintained by what amounted to a longitudinal Watt linkage on each side and by virtue of the 15° splay of each leading and trailing link the axle could not move sideways either. This arrangement works perfectly in a true bounce and rebound situation, but when there is different suspension movement on each side as in the roll condition then the links are in conflict. Such twisting that inevitably occurred was accommodated by the rubber bushes at the ends of the links, but effectively the rear axle acted as a huge anti-roll bar and in the fullness of time the axle tubes have been found to dissociate themselves from the central differential casing in protest. However, this system did work fairly well and only in conditions of severe cornering did the linkage cause the inside rear wheel to leave the ground giving rise to sudden oversteer.

Having dispensed with the Ford leaf springs this only left the Ford rear axle and steering box to be removed from the design. Reliant had a suitable rear axle of their own construction already in use on their three-wheeled commercials which only required suitable brackets to be attached to pick up the leading and trailing links. Larger rear brakes were borrowed from the current Austin A60. Steering by rack and pinion seemed the natural choice, but hardly fitted in with the obligatory front suspension geometry that necessitated the steering track rods to pivot in the same line as the suspension arm fulcrums which when produced met at the centre line of the car ahead of the wheel centres. David Page's ingenious answer to this was to use just half of a rack and pinion system that only one tie rod emerged to meet a bell-crank pivoted at the centre of

Reliant's modified coil-spring suspension systems evolved for the Sabra/Sabre.

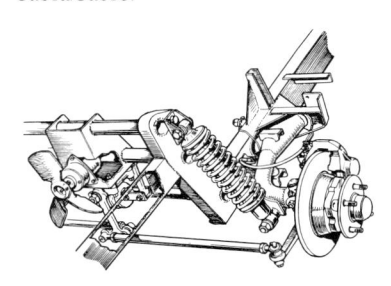

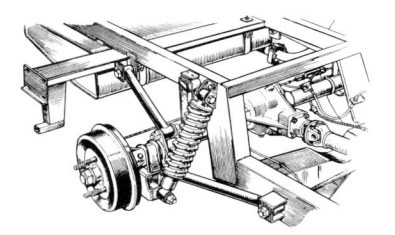

the front crossmember to the other end of which the two steering track rods were jointed. He anticipated quite pronounced steering reaction as a result of the leading arm design so he incorporated provision for a steering damper to act directly on the end of the tie rod from the rack and pinion. This was only partially successful in its desired function by virtue of the reversible nature of the chosen steering mechanism and perhaps in this instance some rather less positive system such as the original recirculating ball steering box might have proved a better compromise.

Ken Wood's methods of persuading the Ashley body to fit the modified Ballamy chassis are less easy to describe; suffice to say they were not that easy to achieve even though the wheelbase more or less matched up on each component. Ashley's only provided moulds for an outer shell with mounting subframes for either the Austin or Ford chassis. These were of little help in the case of the Sabra and though Reliant adopted a complete fibreglass bodyshell in their own three- and four-wheelers, the cost of producing a fibreglass floorpan to fit the existing shell would have exceeded the budget for the operation. The compromise in this case was to use marine plywood encased in fibreglass as the floor material bonded in to the GRP outer shell with a metal hoop around the scuttle structure, also bonded in for additional strength. When it came to the glass, controls and trimmings the principle of rummaging around mass-producers parts bins was used. Reliant did undertake moulding a purpose-built facia panel to incorporate the number of instruments befitting a sporting car including a clock, but the windscreen surmounting this panel was from the Meadows Frisky three-wheeler microcar as the one offered by Ashley was too flat for the purpose. Even more exotic was the insertion of Alfa Romeo Giulietta Sprint rear light units which have proved very difficult to locate in recent years.

Rear view of the Sabra showing the Alfa Romeo Giulietta Sprint rear lights and unhappy square wheel arches.

The Sabra facia was well stocked with instruments and the cactus motif features in the centre of the steering wheel.

By contrast BMC dash and heater controls as well as some door furniture were employed in the Sabra. The interior was fully carpeted and a wood rim Les Leston steering wheel was a nice finishing touch. One feature of the Ashley body which was advanced for the period involved the complete one-piece bonnet and front wing assembly which hinged forward giving unrivalled access to the engine and front suspension. Aston Martin had used this feature earlier as did other contemporaries of the Sabre, the Triumph Herald and Spitfires well known for ease of servicing. Autocars had decided to use the Ford Consul 1703cc engine for the Sabra which caused very few mounting problems since this was anticipated in the Ballamy application of his chassis, but far more surprising was the adoption of the delightful and very expensive ZF S4-12 4-speed gearbox. This unit was only offered in one other British car as an option, namely the Lotus Elite. Perhaps ZF had few applications for the unit and supplied Autocars with them at preferential rates; whatever the reason the result in the car was to make it one of its most desirable features. The compact and lightweight gearbox had no difficulty in coping with the 72bhp produced by the Consul unit which was enhanced to a claimed 90bhp (gross) when fitted with an optional Alexander twin SU modification.

THE SABRE

The front-hinging bonnet provided uninterrupted access to the engine and front suspension.

The Sabra exhibited at the Motor Show alongside the Carmel and Sussita estate car.

Since one of the prime objects of producing the Sabra from Autocars point of view was to eventually export it to the USA to earn dollars for Israel, it seemed entirely appropriate that the car should have its debut in that country. It is a tribute to the British engineers that completed prototypes were available for display at the New York Motor Show in the Spring of 1961 where the three-pronged cactus badge of the Sabra marque first made its appearance before the American public. The speed of development by Reliant was not matched by the preparations by Autocars for assembly of the car from imported kits in Israel. Thus the first 100 Sabras were fully constructed at Tamworth and exported direct to North America on behalf of Autocars in left-hand drive configurations of course. Quite what the financial arrangement was with Autocars is unclear, but this initial production run by Reliant caused Ray Wiggin to speculate on the possibility of producing RHD versions of the Sabra under their own banner for the British market. It proved quite simple to convert a couple of the USA-bound cars to RHD for a trial marketing operation and so chassis nos. 92 and 93 never made their intended destination, but instead appeared on the Reliant stand at the 1961 Motor Show in October, re-christened the Sabre 4 sports. The name change was very subtle yet so fitting for a two seater car which naturally sported its own badge featuring a Sabre prominently. These two pioneering Reliant sports cars (7946 WD and 7947 WD) were released to the press after the show for assessment and fittingly are now reunited in Surrey in the tender care of the Valler family.

The press and public reaction at the Motor Show was a guarded welcome in as much as the concept and potential of the Sabre was undoubtedly attractive, but certain elements of the bodywork were less so, particularly with regard to the frontal appearance. Autocars had decided that the Ashley front was too low and vulnerable for American traffic conditions and since adequate bumpers would have been difficult to mount in front of the already prominent bonnet, two large vertical horn-like overriders were grafted onto each side of the front grille. These appendages looked as if they had been removed from a large transatlantic automobile, particularly as garish chrome coverings adorned them. It was perhaps a shame that Reliant could not have identified their model from the Sabra by omitting the automotive gargoyles for the UK market and have complimented the smooth bonnet line with Perspex covers for the headlamps as on the E-type Jaguar also appearing for the first time at the same exhibition. Bill Boddy, the forthright Editor of 'Motor Sport' was almost unkind when he confided to approximately 100,000 loyal readers "a new sports car was the Reliant Sabre, of which the back axle in the high old-fashioned box-section chassis was described as located by a modified Watt linkage. The technical pundits say it will need a good deal more modification before it will be any good . . . never mind, there is always a dud at every show — last year it was the Lea Francis."

A bare chassis also on display aroused many a comment about the curious front suspension design and the more mathematically minded observers could not fathom out how the rear axle could move in any direction other than a true vertical one. Hardly ever was the idiom 'proof of the pudding is in the eating' more true than in the comments made by correspondents after they had driven the car, when almost universally they reported that it was nothing like as bad as they had feared. Not unexpectedly the ZF gearbox was immediately praised for its light 'switch-like' action between its close ratios which enabled the relatively unsporting Ford Consul engine to

Cutaway diagram of the delightful ZF four-speed gearbox employed by Reliant.

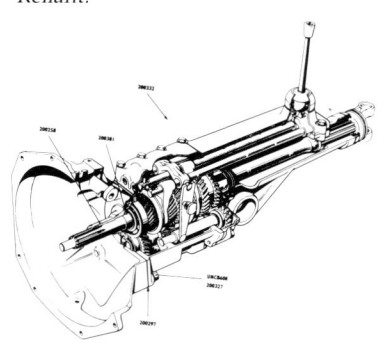

The Sabre

The Sabre on display at Earls Court.

endow the Sabre with a quite sporting performance. Synchromesh on all four gears was another endearing and unusual feature on such a car and a great advantage due to the relatively high gearing when first gear was often needed from slow uphill corners. It was on corners, however, where most testers expected trouble and a similar majority were pleasantly surprised as summed up by the report in 'Autocar' who tested 7946 WD the following March "the practically roll-free suspension allows very fast cornering indeed. Pirelli Cintura tyres play their part in this, giving remarkable powers of adhesion even on wet surfaces, and never drawing attention to the high cornering forces by squealing. At low speeds the suspension is firm, yet not so harsh as that of some current sports cars; it evens out considerably as speed increases and provides comfortable travel on the good metalled roads found in this country. Over special test surfaces of washboard and pavé, however, it was not happy, and over pavé in particular, excessive road wheel reactions were transmitted to the driver's hands. This seems inevitable with the association of highly reversible rack and pinion steering and the Sabre's type of front suspension". When 'Motor' magazine tested 7947 WD they came to similar conclusions on the handling properties of the Sabre and commented "the overall effect was better than we had expected (much better than we feared) and there is only the occasional jerking of the steering wheel in the driver's hands during most British driving, rather than any sort of incessant vibration. In-built friction damping at the

The front bumper 'horns' spoilt a potentially pleasing bonnet line.

steering rack can unfortunately conceal the self-centring action of the front wheels at town speeds, but at speed the Sabre proves perfectly stable and needs the minimum of conscious guidance". The latter car was fitted with the optional hard top which along with the Microcell seats and wire wheels were the only options available. This hard top accentuated the narrowness of the cockpit and some of the squeaks and rattles that inevitably emanate from a pre-production prototype such as the cars being tested. However, in summarising their opinions the Sabre was considered to have good handling, adequate performance and economy, was fun to drive and distinctive, but expensive compared with its competitors. The performance comparision with some of the Sabre's competitors is outlined below:

	Sabre 4	MGA	Alpine	TVR
Capacity (cc)	1,703	1,588	1,592	1,588
Power (bhp)	72	79.5	85	79.5
Max speed (mph)	93.7	100	96.7	98.4
0-60 mph (secs)	14.4	13.3	13.6	12.0
Standing ¼ mile	19.9	19.3	19.7	19.0
mpg (overall)	27	24	26	24
Weight (cwt)	16¼	18¼	19¾	15
Price (£)	1,164	940	986	1,298

This table highlights the price handicap of the Sabre 4 when studying the brochures apart from that of its frontal appearance in the showroom. In order to try and offset these handicaps and bring the performance on a par with the best in its class, Reliant offered a twin SU carburettor option developed by Alexander Engineering of

Haddenham for the Ford engine which boosted the gross bhp to a claimed 90 giving the car a true 100mph potential for the modest sum of £52.

The result of this brave entry into the critical sports car market was a mere 55 cars sold in the UK during the two years it was in production compared with a total of 153 complete cars exported making a total run of 208 cars. This does not include about 50 kits which were eventually exported to Israel for local assembly. Few of these kits ever found their way on to the roads of Haifa as Autocars went into liquidation in 1963 and most of the Tamworth products were impounded by Customs and Excise in Tel Aviv on account of this. Only as recently as 1980 did these kits emerge when they were auctioned off by the Israeli government and from them only about six ZF gearboxes were rescued and returned privately to the UK where they were eagerly snapped up by Sabre and Lotus Elite enthusiasts for handsome sums of money.

Ray Wiggin had infectious enthusiasm for the Sabre and would listen patiently to the oft-repeated moans about the car's deficiencies only to quell all argument among his colleagues by gently pointing out that there were hundreds of front suspension leading arms in store which had to be used up. The reactions of the motor trade ranged from polite interest to indifference or even derision and a director of one of the country's largest sports car retailers described the Sabre as "the most expensive Ford special ever built".

Sabres in production at Tamworth.

Perhaps the Reliant advertising copywriters did not assist greatly when they suggested that "piloting the new Sabre sports is a startling experience", no doubt referring to the aeroplane-like instrument panel, but possibly anticipating its steering reaction to bumpy roads in the eyes of cynical observers who found it sufficiently spiteful to cut a finger resting on an alloy spoke of the steering wheel.

Not everyone was quite so scathing including one Ken Dodd who bought one from Argyll Motors in Birkenhead, while he was appearing at Blackpool, and confessed to being thrilled with his new toy.

Despite these setbacks at home and abroad, Reliant were undaunted and the management were even persuaded to enter works-built and supported cars in international rallies. This highlighted some additional weaknesses in the Sabre as well as hastening the development of the fixed head version which was made available towards the end of the production run. The Americans were disturbed by the poor sales across the Atlantic too and Ray Wiggin visited Reg Wayne in the USA, who bought the first consignment of Sabras to assess the problem and concluded that more power and better appearance were the two areas for urgent attention. The same conclusions also obtained on the home market and the logical source of more power was the 6 cylinder Ford engine as fitted to the Zephyr and Zodiac models. This engine used identical mountings, but, due to its greater length, the special steering rack now had to be re-positioned ahead of the front axle line. While adopting the larger

New Sabre 6 chassis on display at the Motor Show showing the doomed 'flailing-arm' front suspension and the floor gearchange adaptation to the Zodiac MkIII gearbox.

The Sabre

engine Reliant also fitted the Zodiac overdrive gearbox to which Reliant added its own remote floor change which was necessary in a sports car. This must have reduced costs as well as providing better servicing facilities for the owners even though the quality of the gearchange was inferior to the ZF predecessor. Reliant's engineers wisely decided to abandon their basically three-wheeler rear axle in view of the 109bhp produced by this larger engine and bought-in a Salisbury 7HA unit with suitable bracketry to accommodate the peculiar rear suspension arrangement. Naturally, higher rated springs and shock absorbers were specified and the rest of the chassis was beefed-up by means of a cruciform member amidships to clear the long Ford gearbox extension with a detachable crossmember to carry the latter component. The front chassis extensions were more widely spaced to accommodate a four-row Lawrence radiator and two extra body-mounting outriggers sprouted from either side of the main chassis rails. The brakes were considered adequate for the heavier, faster car and so remained unaltered.

It was naturally desirable to give the new car, to be known as the Sabre 6 or SE2 model (SE being derived from the first and last letters from Sabre) a different and hopefully improved appearance from its 4 cylinder brother. Ray Wiggin was very friendly with Edward Eves of 'Autocar' magazine (no connection with the Israeli firm I should add) and accepted his advice that the front of the bonnet should be shortened for aesthetic and functional reasons. The detail work on the bodywork alterations was undertaken by Colin Thompson from designs by Eddie Pepall in the drawing office. The result of the axe job on the front end shortened the car by 7in and gave a much improved frontal aspect, not unlike the later MGB with the addition

Short-nose Sabre 4 drophead publicity car, now residing in Northern Ireland.

The new fastback Coupé design was marred by the dummy roof vent and the rather abrupt rear panel.

of a power bulge down the centre of the new bonnet to enhance the effect. Eddie also finalised the fixed head shape first seen on one of the first rally cars (15 CUE) which featured a fastback roofline merging into the existing boot area with a curious circular rear window. To match the front profile he now cut the back off at a vertical angle, but finished up with an awkward angular rear aspect without any attempt to blend the roofline and wing shape to cater for the shorter tail. He did manage, however, to find a far more ready source of rear light units to match the new shape from the Farina Austin A40. The crude square rear wheel arches were now rounded off which greatly improved the profile of the car which was now not unlike the Triumph GT6 that followed a couple of years later. The two remaining flaws from this aspect were the angles of the windscreen and front edge of the rear wings. To alter either would have involved rather more drastic and expensive changes to doors and window glass, which could not be justified.

The Sabre 6 was ready for the October 1962 Motor Show and

The Sabre

The fixed head bodywork did little to improve the appearance of the Sabre 4.

similar body modifications were incorporated gradually into the Sabre 4 range which continued in production alongside the more powerful model. The fixed head option was available from chassis no. 130 although the bulk of the cars produced were still in open form, by contrast only two open versions of the Sabre 6 ever left the factory. The short bonnet, however, was only fitted to the last eight Sabre 4's produced (chassis no. 201-208), although many earlier cars acquired these later mouldings in the course of time either by choice of the owners or because of an accident. Only 17 examples of the Sabre 6 had been produced when it was obvious to the engineers and testers of these early cars that the handling was now totally unacceptable and that the 'flailing-arm' front suspension (as it became known) was a quite inadequate means of locating the front wheels of such a fast and nose-heavy machine. As a result of suggestions from Edward Eves among others, it was decided to remove the semi-swing axles altogether and graft on the double wishbone system produced by Alford and Alder for the Triumph TR4. This proved remarkably straightforward as both cars used a ladder type chassis at the front and re-jigging of the front chassis extension and crossmember allowed the Triumph Herald steering rack to fit perfectly. At last the Sabre was blessed with a front suspension capable of giving the car safe and predictable handling. The scar of the earlier Ballamy design is present on every subsequent Sabre as the original chassis pressings were still used and the leading link pivot location then had to be blanked off when these pressings were welded together.

The press were suitably impressed with the results of this transplant and the 'Autocar' tester commented "on twisting main

One of the two Sabre 6 dropheads produced.

The Sabre 6 on test by 'Autocar' looked very imposing from the front.

The hardtop was a rare optional extra for the dropheads.

roads its almost neutral steering allows it to be really hustled through corners, a very slight oversteer setting in when the limit is approached. These good road manners are undoubtedly helped by the Pirelli Cintura tyres, which give most impressive grip both in the wet and dry". The 'Motor' correspondent has similar views about the behaviour of the front end and the Italian tyres, but still had reservations about the rear suspension when he stated "at low speeds on coarse surfaces the back end does wander slightly — not enough to require steering correction, but enough to be felt. Once the power is turned on, with the rubber bushes compressed in the right direction, it feels fine, although this and its susceptibility to side winds may well be due to a lack of a Panhard rod or similar link. Suspension travel is limited at the rear by the axle casing acting as an anti-roll bar when one wheel takes a bump, making the whole car feel rigid and overdamped." The straight line performance of the Sabre 6 was now fully competitive even if it still suffered a slight handicap when it came to price as the table below illustrates:

	Sabre 6	TR4	Healey 3000	MGB
Capacity (cc)	2,553	1,991	2,912	1,798
Power (bhp)	109	105	150	95
Max speed (mph)	109	109	122	108
0-60mph (secs)	9.9	10.9	10.3	12.1
Standing ¼ mile	17.6	18.1	17.3	18.7
mpg (overall)	23.5	24.0	17.5	23.0
Weight (cwt)	19¾	19½	21¾	18½
Price (£)	1,136	958	1166	834

There was no lack of instruments in the Sabre 6, but it was not always easy to see them from the driving seat. Wooden-rim steering wheel was a pleasant feature.

Despite the major improvements made to the car compared with the 4 cylinder model only 77 cars left Tamworth during the two years it was in production of which only one — the last example — was exported to Europe. The overdrive gearbox certainly gave the Sabre 6 good touring properties with 26mph per 1,000rpm in overdrive top, but the car lacked the refinement of comfort, space and silence to take maximum advantage of its undoubted dynamic abilities. Aesthetics also played their part as the body shape still left something to be desired and the interior styling around the fascia was not to everyone's taste, neither was the finish of the cabin. The same cannot be said, however, of the fibreglass bodywork which was of a very good standard with accurate shut lines and a very solid feel when

The Sabre

Cliff Richard, the Shadows and showbusiness contemporaries on a visit to Reliant.

travelling inside the car. John Bolster in 'Autosport' summed up the Sabre by saying that "it has made great progress since the Consul engined machine with swing axles at the front. It has now reached a stage where it has some most likeable features and needs a little further development before it becomes really competitive. To take on the giant combines with one relatively small factory is courageous indeed." William Boddy of 'Motor Sport' was far less generous with his final appraisal when he wrote "we found the Sabre to be a lot better than we feared and if Reliant build a sports car starting with a clean sheet of paper it could be very good indeed".

Norman in his wisdom actually bought a Sabre 6 for personal use!

    The Sabre 6 nevertheless appealed to some show business personalities, namely Norman Wisdom and Danny Williams, both of whom followed Ken Dodd's example by purchasing their Sabres from Argyll Motors.

    Then came the courageous decision of Reliant and Ray Wiggin in particular to tackle international rallies when a brutal comparison could be drawn between the Sabre and its mass-produced and extensively developed competitors. Surprisingly, they were not put to shame as we shall see in the next chapter and much was learned from this brave exercise. Undoubtedly there was an abundance of enthusiasm within the company at that time determined to make the new venture succeed and they were always willing to listen to advice from experts and act on this when possible.

Sabres in rallying

out of the tough, relentless world of international rallies emerges the performance proved

SEE THE Sabre Six at the following showrooms

Success in Europe's toughest rallies has proved the outstanding qualities of the Sabre Six — the car that combines distinctive elegance and unusual luxury with the high performance, reliability and roadholding of a truly great car.

BERKSHIRE
Cottage Pie (Motors) Ltd.,
Lordon Road, Twyford.

BUCKINGHAMSHIRE
Venture Car Sales, Aylesbury Street.
C. G. (Bletchley) Ltd., Bletchley.

CAMBRIDGESHIRE
Empress Garage, Park Street, Chatteris.

CHESHIRE
Argyle Motors (Birkenhead) Ltd.,
12-14 Conway Street, Birkenhead.

DERBYSHIRE
Motorway Sales (Derby) Ltd.,
Station Approach, Friargate, Derby.

GLOUCESTERSHIRE
Three Cocks Motors,
Barton Street, Gloucester.

HAMPSHIRE
Morgan Rees Motors Ltd.,
93-97 Park Road, Farnborough.

HERTFORDSHIRE
J. Dixon & Son Ltd.,
High Wych Garage, Sawbridgeworth.

ISLE OF WIGHT
P. V. Pritchett Ltd.,
Hunnyhill Garage, Newport.

KENT
Frank Bannister & Son Ltd.,
26 Railway Street, Chatham.

LANCASHIRE
McIntyre's Garages,
Bury Road, Tonge Fold, Bolton.

LEICESTERSHIRE
Jones' Garage Ltd.,
Mexton Road, Syston, Leicester.

LINCOLNSHIRE
Long Sutton Motors,
London Road, Long Sutton.

LONDON
The Chequered Flag
(Sports Car Specialists) Ltd.,
492-496 High Road, Chiswick, W.4.

NORTHAMPTONSHIRE
Venture Filling Station,
Watling Street, Paulerspury,
(near) Towcester.

NOTTINGHAMSHIRE
The Chequered Flag (Midland) Ltd.,
Arkwright Street, Nottingham.

OXFORDSHIRE
J. H. Willock,
Middleton Cheney, Banbury.

SOMERSET
Alexandre Motors (Sandford) Ltd.,
Fourways Garage, Sandford, (near) Bristol.

STAFFORDSHIRE
Bilston Motor Mart,
High Street, Bilston.

SUFFOLK
The Steering Wheel,
Out Eastgate Street, Bury St. Edmunds.

SURREY
Morgan Rees Motors Ltd.,
London Road, Blackwater, Camberley.

SUSSEX
E. P. I. Cars (St. Leonards) Ltd.,
12a Eastern Street, St. Leonards-on-Sea.

WORCESTERSHIRE
Talbot Garage Co. (Stourbridge) Ltd.,
Talbot Street, Stourbridge.

YORKSHIRE
Frank Leach Motors Ltd.,
Manor Garage, Headingley Lane,
Leeds 6.

or write direct for brochure

RELIANT MOTOR CO. LIMITED, Two Gates, Tamworth, Staffordshire

CHAPTER 3

Sabres in rallying

MANY OF THE developments in the history of the Sabre seem to have been promoted by chance external influences rather than well thought out advance policies on the part of the Board. This does not infer any reluctance on the part of Reliant to pursue these proposals which, in most cases, they followed up keenly. It was in such a manner that the company first became involved in competition motoring. Within six months of the Sabre 4 announcement the Board of Reliant were becoming unhappy about the car as they doubtless began to realise its shortcomings. As a result, early in March 1962, Ray Wiggin consulted his managerial colleagues for suggestions on improving the Sabre's prospects. What appeared to be the most ludicrous suggestion came from Arthur Rusling whose task within the company was to try and sell the car to the trade outlets. With tongue in cheek after listing a number of modifications he would like to see introduced immediately, he put in a plea for an entry for the Le Mans endurance race due to be run in June. He considered the long-legged gearing would enable the Sabre to give a fairly high speed demonstration which could not fail to assist its development and materially assist the sales effort from the incalculable prestige such a race would give. Furthermore the surface of Le Mans was so smooth that it should not create any suspension or steering problems for the drivers. Perhaps mercifully for Reliant's reputation the entry list for the race was already closed, but Arthur Rusling was astonished to be asked to attend the Board room shortly afterwards to comment on the desirability of entering a Sabre 4 in the forthcoming Tulip International Rally. The suggestion had emanated from an experienced rally driver, Peter Easton, who happened to be the Public Relations consultant to Reliant. Arthur was even offered the task of co-driver, which must have caused him a full fraction of a second's delay before he answered in the affirmative, as he was no newcomer to motor sport, mainly concerned with racing and hill climbing and one or two club rallies.

The first problem was the need to homologate the Sabre 4 with the RAC within the seven weeks before the event, as well as prepare a suitable car. Quite how Arthur persuaded the authorities that 100 identical examples had been produced within the previous 12 months, with the tuning modifications incorporated and in a record five weeks, we shall never know. Bob Munro, then in charge of Sabre production, undertook the responsibility of preparing a suitable car which, in the interests of comfort and safety, was destined to be a fixed head version despite the inevitable weight penalty. The final result, with a sweeping fastback and circular window, was almost as ugly as the horns adorning the bonnet, making the whole car look horrendous and a testimony to the lack of stylists within the company. The engine was selectively assembled by Ford and to Arthur's consternation produced all of 57bhp on the test bed, so

Arthur Rusling overlooking the prototype rally Sabre 4 with its peculiar round rear window.

Alexander Engineering were given the opportunity of breathing on it by increasing the compression ratio from 7.8 to 8.9, fitting larger exhaust valves and two SU carburettors. Even then it did not realise the claimed 90bhp, but at least gave the car a genuine maximum speed of around the then magic 100mph, which might just keep them in sight of the slower TR4s and MGAs in the 2-litre class. Naturally, a few extra navigational instruments and a couple of spotlights were fitted. The production team had done an excellent job in completing 15 CUE in time for it to be run-in by Arthur, Peter Easton, Tom Scott (Sales Director) and Bob Aston, the Mintex Competitions Manager who supplied the brake linings. The crew were not confident of a good result in the rally with such a power deficiency, nevertheless Peter found he was reasonably competitive on flat but twisty sections due to what he described as "its superb road-holding and light steering, which however lacked self-centring". On the hills the lack of power and the high gearing were a problem, even though the ZF gearbox was a joy to use and the car cruised easily in the 80s on the more open sections. Sadly they had to retire because Peter fell ill during the event, causing them to lose time, but they still completed the course to prove that the car was capable of such a task, which it did without any mechanical maladies. Arthur Rusling was very encouraged by this fact and after this Rally set his sights on the RAC Rally later in 1962.

Sabres In Rallying

The experiences on the Tulip highlighted the need for more power and a lower axle ratio as well as some added lightness to make the Sabre more competitive. Luckily Arthur Rusling had taken the advice of Michael Christie from Alexander Engineering to homologate the car with alternative lower ratios of 3.9:1 and 4.375:1, so that solved one problem. The Sussex firm of Nerus were given the opportunity of further tuning the engines, resulting in a still unspectacular 77bhp. Meanwhile Arthur tackled a couple of club rallies in 15 CUE with his friend David Goad, to gain more experience of the Sabre in competition, with no great success. He also invited Peter Riley, then a BMC works driver in a Healey 3000, to try the Sabre in central Wales. Peter immediately proved his predictions of a first inspection by removing the radiator and holing the fuel tank in a very short distance of determined driving, but pointed out to Ray Wiggin that these problems could be overcome and Reliant would gain much prestige by participating in the RAC Rally in November. The enthusiastic deputy fuhrer hardly needed such encouragement and ordered the preparation of a team of three Sabre 4s for the event based on the new fixed head designs drawn up by Eddie Pepall, one of which would be 15 CUE suitably rebuilt. The new pair were

Jimmy Ray and John Hopwood on the 1962 RAC Rally.

registered 6 EUE and 7 EUE. The search was then on for experienced drivers, with the first lead coming from one of Reliant's energetic distributors, Argyle Motors of Birkenhead. They had been approached by Jimmy Ray, previous winner of the RAC in 1955 driving a Standard, to borrow a Sabre for the RAC. Arthur had soon recruited him into the team as his previous successes with Triumph and Rootes would be of great assistance to the inexperienced Reliant Equipe. Jimmy accepted after trying the Sabre in Wales, where he admitted that the car could barely keep up with the current high-flying Ford Anglias and he elected to have John Hopwood as his co-driver. Another Lancashire driver Derrick Astle, who had shared a Healey 3000 with Peter Riley, was invited to drive the second car accompanied by Peter Roberts. The team was completed by 'Motoring News' Championship winner Tony Fisher who nominated John King to sit in the hot seat. A further approach to borrow a car came from Arthur's friend from Mintex, Bob Aston, who was keen to compete in the RAC with Gerald Cooper. Ray Wiggin agreed and an open two seater about to be scrapped from the Development Department (42 ENX) was requisitioned and fitted with a hard top for Bob to enter privately with the promise of works service support. Pre-rally testing took place at Oulton Park with a standard production two seater and as an indication of future plans a prototype 6 cylinder version was also present, in which Derrick Astle became particularly keen and demonstrated its potential by lapping a full 4mph quicker than the 4 cylinder model.

Arthur Rusling proudly surveying the prototype Sabre 6.

Two works Sabre 4's undergoing preparation for the RAC Rally.

The RAC Rally was altogether tougher than the Tulip and though Derrick Astle was lying an incredibly good fifth overall after eight stages, including 75 miles of forestry tracks, the pounding soon began to take its toll, particularly in the area of the rear suspension. In trials, frequent bottoming had been experienced, so bump stops were placed above the centre of the axle casing. Not unexpectedly during the rally itself continual pounding in this area distorted the axle casings, causing the retirement of both Derrick and Tony early in the event. Jimmy Ray and John Hopwood were not without their problems when on one rough Yorkshire stage the windscreen fell into their laps quite intact and they had to resort to taping it in place for the rest of the event. Later they holed the fuel tank, but when the service crew attempted to replace it they found that the new bodywork had been moulded round it so a loose tank behind the seats was the only, potentially explosive, remedy. They also had some axle troubles, but battled on to finish in 38th position out of 102 finishers, four places behind the privately entered car of Bob Aston and Gerry Cooper. Despite their troubles and criticisms of the cars Derrick and Jimmy were very keen to stay in the team for the 1963 Monte Carlo Rally in two months' time.

It was now obvious that more organisation was going to be needed as the service crew had been hopelessly overworked on the RAC and so a Competition Department was formed with Arthur Rusling as Secretary with overall responsibility for the cars and personnel. He firstly recruited a team of three mechanics comprising Martin Routledge and Ken Chatwin from the Development Department and Lai Parkes, a first-class engineer from the maintenance section. Coincidentally, Mintex were known to be withdrawing from the competition field, which made Bob Aston an obvious choice to run the team directly in view of his good showing in the RAC Rally. A new building was provided for the rally car preparation under Bob's control, but only a fortnight before the start of the Monte Carlo Rally, so much feverish work took place in the early part of January 1963. Three cars were entered from the Glasgow start with the following crews:

No. 139	Derrick Astle/Peter Roberts	(6 EUE)
No. 156	Jimmy Ray/Michael Hughes	(42 ENX)
No. 172	Tony Fisher/David Skeffington	(7 EUE)

Derrick Astle and Peter Roberts at a control on the 1963 Monte Carlo Rally.

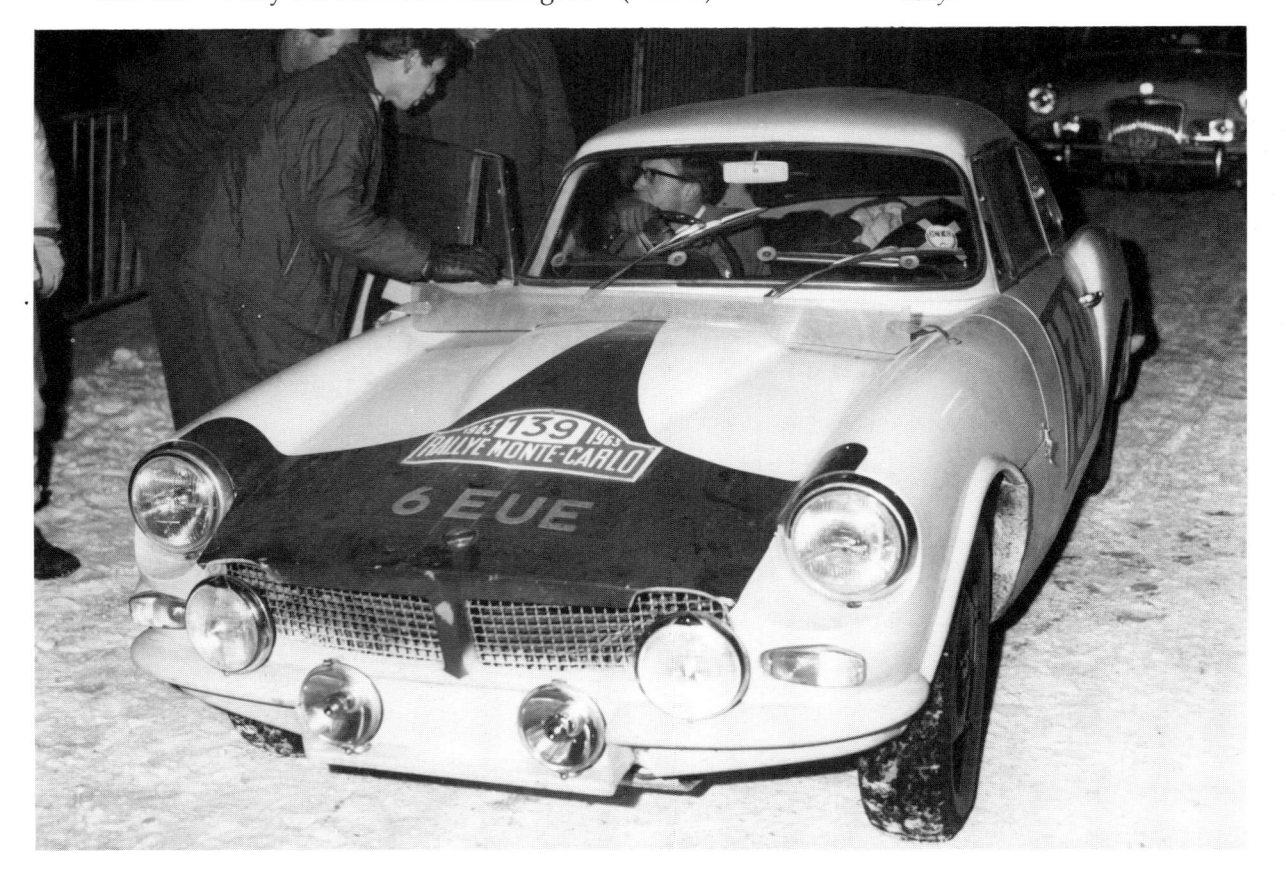

Sabres In Rallying

Derrick Astle cornering on the Monte Carlo circuit test in 1963.

Tony Fisher and David Skeffington on a snow-bound section of the 1963 Monte.

Supporting these competitors were Bob Aston and Martin Routledge (15 CUE), Arthur Rusling and Barry Twell in another Sabre 4 (187 DWD) and finally Ken Chatwin and Lai Parkes in a five year old Zephyr Farnham estate car. Following the rally on a proving run, but not competing, was a newly introduced Regal 3/25 three-wheeler driven by David Cooper, Press Officer of the British Cycle and Motorcycle Association and Cecil Sandford, former 125cc and 250cc Motorcycle World Champion.

Rear suspension bottoming was still a problem with the rally cars so en route from the Glasgow start to Dover they called in at the factory for stiffer springs to be fitted. The weather was notoriously bad that winter and snow covered most of the routes to Monte Carlo with many resulting incidents. Jimmy Ray first clouted a very solid church in France, losing his lights and some fibreglass, so when they met up with the support crews the entire bonnet was replaced with the one off 187 DWD, leaving Arthur and Barry to sort out their own illumination. Later Jimmy slid off the Col du Turini and had to retire. The first seven places in the rally were taken by front wheel drive cars, helped by the slippery conditions, but Derrick and Tony completed the route to finish third and fourth in the 2-litre class some

Two works Sabre 4's back in the Two Gates workshop at Tamworth.

Sabres In Rallying

way behind Walter's Porsche and Thuner's TR4 and were two of only ten Glasgow finishers, plus the gallant, unofficial Regal. While at Monte Carlo, John Davenport, then 'Verglas' of 'Motoring News', arranged with Arthur to test the highest placed Sabre 4 when they were back in England and his summary of the trial was "in all the Reliant went well and possessed many features which may eventually cause it to mature into a successful rally car. It is certainly refreshing to see a small private firm building a new car and entering it in rallies for development purposes." The writing was truly on the wall for the underpowered and undeveloped Sabre 4 and Arthur Rusling was now looking to the 6 cylinder car as a means of chasing the large manufacturers in the rallying scene. The last outing of a works Sabre 4 was a lone entry by Tony Fisher in the Circuit of Ireland Rally with Ron Crellin and a Sabre 6 tender car driven by Reg Darlington. They came a creditable third in class, after which the three works cars were sold off, being advertised for £700 each. One of these cars (42 ENX) was purchased by Leslie Griffiths, a Reliant agent at Alexandre Motors near Bristol and was to appear again alongside the later Sabre 6 models.

Alex Griffiths with his father Leslie and their ex-works Sabre 4 at their Bristol Garage.

It took little persuasion for Ray Wiggin to allow four of the new cars to be allocated to the Competitions Department (nos. SS300109/110/111/112) for modification into one race car and three rally cars respectively, for possible entries in the 1963 Le Mans Race and Alpine Rally in June. Derrick Astle was very keen on the prospects and was loaned the prototype (493 EUE) to develop to his own ideas for circuit racing to replace his Austin Healey 3000 which he had campaigned to good effect. The engines of the Sabre 6s were to be fitted with a Raymond Mays alloy 12-port cylinder head, lightened pistons and three twin-choke Weber carburettors like the Healey opposition from BMC. With such power and the increased weight it was clear the front suspension system would be potentially lethal, but the Reliant Development Department wanted six months to devise a suitable alternative. Equally Ray Wiggin was reluctant to abandon all those leading arms still in store. The Competitions Department only had four months to complete these new cars from scratch, so within seven days they had grafted a TR4 wishbone IFS system on to the front of the hack Sabre 4 (15 CUE) which at once transformed the handling of the car and removed all the painful kick-back in the steering. The same principle was immediately incorporated into the rally 6s, allied to a Triumph Spitfire based steering rack. The rear suspension was not altered, but a stronger Salisbury 7HA axle was now used with a low 4.1:1 ratio with disc brakes at each end borrowed from the Aston Martin DB4 and also used on the Daimler SP250 sports car. Jaguar

Bobby Parkes and Gerry Cooper in the class-winning Sabre 6 on the 1963 Alpine Rally.

SABRES IN RALLYING

overdrive gearboxes were homologated into the specification to handle the anticipated 175bhp and twin circuit un-servoed brakes fitted for safety reasons. The bodywork now incorporated steel roll-over protection tubes moulded into the B-pillars and roof, which probably saved the lives of two crew members later in the car's career. The vulnerable fuel tank was now placed above the rear axle, with the spare wheel on top behind the occupants' shoulders inside the cabin. The windscreens were now laminated whereas the rest of the glass was replaced with Perspex for lightness. Since there was not time to homologate the new cars in time for the Tulip Rally, Derrick Astle was released to take part in his own Healey 3000, only to be tragically killed in an accident in France, leaving a much lamented vacuum in the Reliant team.

Arthur Rusling had already enrolled Bobby Parkes to replace Tony Fisher in the team and was now on the lookout for another experienced driver to occupy the seat Derrick had been so looking forward to filling. After talking in vain to Timo Makinen and Tom Trana, he entered an up-and-coming young driver, one Roger Clark, in his first ever works drive, with Bob Aston to keep an eye on him from the navigator's seat. So the line-up consisted of:

Roger Clark on his first ever works drive and the only time he drove for Reliant coming 2nd-in-Class on the 1963 Alpine Rally.

No. 1	Jimmy Ray/Peter Roberts	(648 GUE)
No. 2	Roger Clark/Bob Aston	(650 GUE)
No. 3	Bobby Parkes/Gerry Cooper	(649 GUE)

These were up against the formidable Austin Healey 3000s of Morley, Hopkirk and Makinen and of course no one gave Reliant a chance in that company. A lone private entry by Leslie Griffiths in 42 ENX gave moral support to the works trio. The new 6 cylinder cars were beset with misfiring above 4,500rpm right from the start due to wrong fuel mixture settings, yet in the early stages of the Alpine Rally the three works cars occupied 3rd, 4th and 5th places in the over 2,500cc class, which raised their hopes somewhat. Gradually Roger Clark was acclimatising himself to the peculiar handling of his new steed after the predictable feel of his previous Cortina GT mount and was occasionally recording stage times in the top ten. Fortunes were soon to change when Jimmy Ray did it again and slid off the road, damaging the rear axle against a tree enforcing his retirement. Even greater misfortune hit the BMC camp when both leading Healeys succumbed to failures, giving the remaining two Sabre 6s the top positions in their class on a plate. The drivers were now urged to nurse their rough-sounding cars to the finish, which they succeeded in doing, to achieve creditable 20th and 22nd positions overall for Bobby and Roger respectively and a Coupé des Alpes for a class win. A certain amount of luck, and a great deal of hard work by the service crews, enabled Reliant to record such good results, confirming Ray Wiggin's wisdom in rushing Arthur to get the Sabres ready for the

---

more Sabre successes!!
Alpine Rally 1st and 2nd
(OVER 2½ LITRE G.T. CATEGORY)
Subject to Official Confirmation

Why do Reliant take part in tough International rallies?

Because we believe that if a car will stand up to the pounding and buffeting (and they do you know) of a really tough event — whether on a craggy Alpine Pass or through Scottish mud and slime or over hundreds of miles of sheet ice and snow — when time is all important — the lessons learned will ensure that a quality of inbred toughness will be built into the production models.

And this is happening to the Sabre

For further details please write to:

The Reliant Engineering Co. (Tamworth) Ltd.
Watling Street, Two Gates,
Tamworth, Staffordshire.

SABRE SIX BY RELIANT

event against his better judgement. However, the drivers were very disappointed in the performance of the new cars due to the carburation problems, so Ken Chatwin drove Bobby's class winning car to the Weber factory in Bologna for a short course in tuning their products. Roger Clark was quite outspoken about the Sabre when he wrote later "just about everything was basically wrong with it as a rally car, it was the slowest 2.6-litre car I have ever driven".

Naturally the mood in the Tamworth Competition Department was now buoyant and the next plan to enter the three cars in the Spa-Sofia-Liege Marathon de la Route can only be attributed to almost blind optimism. For this was an extremely rough rally covering long distances which would certainly not suit the Sabre's crude suspension and cramped cockpit. However, a driver search was on again as Roger had moved on to Rover 2000s following his comments about the Sabre and Jimmy Ray did not feel he had the ability to extract the full potential of the car — who did, thought Arthur and what was its potential? Two well known BBC commentators were the next subjects to experience the Sabre's potential in the shape of Raymond Baxter and Robin Richards, making up the following crews:

No. 6	Bobby Parkes/Arthur Senior	(649 GUE)
No. 7	Raymond Baxter/Doug Wilson-Spratt	(648 GUE)
No. 114	Robin Richards/Alec Lobb	(650 GUE)

Raymond Baxter piloting his doomed Sabre 6 on the Spa-Sofia-Liege Marathon.

A full-house works Rally Sabre 6 engine with triple 48 DCOE Webers.

Bobby and Doug used the now veteran 15 CUE as a recce car for the event and for the first time its rear suspension actually broke, so rough were the roads in Yugoslavia. The service crew could do little at that stage to strengthen the cars, only make sure all nuts were split-pinned to prevent them coming loose under the pounding about to be received in the rally. The carburation was still not quite right and was only cured when 'Wilkie' Wilkinson of BRM was prevailed upon to come over and patiently devise suitable jet settings for the three 45 DCOE Webers, allowing the engines to rev smoothly to 6,000rpm and release their full performance. This the drivers put to full use on the autobahns and autoputs, so much so that Bobby Parkes hit a wolf at about 100mph near Belgrade, but only damaged his lights in the process, such was the strength of the fibreglass bodywork of these cars. Quite predictably the rough terrain broke Reliant's lucky run in rallying, and its cars too, and all three cars were out of the Marathon before Titograd, although Raymond Baxter's retirement was the result of an accident rather than mechanical failure, which was probably imminent.

After the rally Raymond wrote to Arthur explaining the cause of the accident and summing up his feelings about the car in his usual eloquent manner "at the time of the accident we had only lost three minutes, but the left hand headlight had fallen out, the right hand fog lamp had fallen off, we had no brakes at all at the first push and the rear suspension was bottoming on almost every bump. I frankly don't consider that the car would have lasted very much longer. Doug and I were very disappointed indeed, because the engine itself was certainly the finest I have ever handled in any competition. However the suspension throughout left a great deal to be desired. The springs were entirely unsuitable for rough going. On the smooth we were as quick as anyone, but the rough stuff was intensely hard work which was not eased by the inadequacy of the headlights, the fact that we were soaked when it rained and could only breathe through a handkerchief in the dust. I thought of sending you the undervest I was wearing at the time to illustrate the latter point, but it seemed to me entirely too unhygienic to put in the post. I consider that the car as it was could have won an event like the Tulip given sufficient courage and luck, but that it was totally unsuitable in every way for this particular event".

Arthur Rusling was well aware of the deficiencies of the rear suspension, now highlighted by the vast improvement brought about by the revised front suspension, but there was little he could do to cure its bad habits without a radical re-design and re-homologation of the car. All he could do before the RAC Rally, which was next in the programme of events, was to soften the springs again. 648 GUE was too badly damaged from its accident in Yugoslavia to be made ready for the British rally, despite having been driven back 1,700 miles following local repairs to the front end. Thus only two works cars appeared at the Blackpool start, driven by the ever loyal Bobby Parkes, now alongside Roy Dixon and, undeterred by his Balkan experience, Raymond Baxter accompanied by Ernest MacMillen. A A similar number of privately entered Sabres boosted the Reliant presence, driven by Leslie Griffiths' son Alex in 42 ENX and another Sabre dealer, Graham Warner of the Steering Wheel Garage in Bury St. Edmunds, in Sabre 6 (WGV 287). Raymond Baxter had the misfortune to retire again when a burst tyre caused the car to land in a ditch and Graham Warner's first run ended with failed electrics. The other two soldiered on, slowly in the rough sections and moderately fast on the smooth ones; even then on one particular yump in the Kielder forest the windscreens of both cars landed on the occupants' laps, much to the amusement of the local marshals. More serious was the failure of an engine main bearing in Bobby's car, which he then had to coax through eight more tough stages before meeting up with the service crew at the half-way halt back at Blackpool. The delay involved in fetching and fitting the new part dropped them back to 92nd out of the 112 cars still running, while Alex Griffiths in the Sabre 4 was 79th. However, Bobby Parkes' skill in nursing the sick car meant they were still in the rally and even though he was limited to using 5,000rpm to assist the new bearing he managed to work up to a final 64th place overall, one place ahead of Alex Griffiths and gaining 3rd in class in the process. The service crews were now beginning to show a degree of professionalism by the manner in which they kept the largely unsuitable cars running in such a tough event.

Ray Wiggin again insisted that they should enter the 1964 Monte Carlo Rally, although the competition staff had little affection for this prestigious event. Since Arthur was also Public Relations Officer for Reliant he could not argue with the publicity consideration for the decision. Bearing in mind the earlier criticisms by the drivers of the inadequate lighting of the Sabres, a further pair of 7in iodine headlamps were grafted on to the bonnets of the three cars, rather like the parallel modifications to the works Healey 3000's. This gave the GUE trio a very ungainly, if purposeful, frontal appearance. Bobby Parkes and Peter Roberts were sent off to do the Welsh Rally in the now rebuilt 648 GUE to test these lights and give the car a shake down run before the Monte, only 14 days away. The works drivers found themselves in the same over 1,600cc class as Alex Griffiths, again in the underpowered 4 cylinder car, and were somewhat shocked to be beaten by the young Bristol driver by one place. He achieved 13th overall and a class win, leaving the works Sabre 6 2nd in class, which at least looked good for the marque. It should be mentioned that Alex Griffiths had previously won this event in his Healey 3000, so was familiar with the terrain and its demands.

The new four-headlight modification grafted on to the Sabre bonnet which hardly improved their appearance even though the four halogen lights enhanced night visibility.

Sabres In Rallying

Bobby Parkes on the 1964 Welsh Rally when they were beaten into 2nd-in-Class by Alex Griffiths in his Sabre 4.

Bobby Parkes pausing on the 1964 Monte Carlo Rally before their big drop!

One further modification made to the works cars in the few days after the Welsh sortie involved fitting 4.6:1 Powerlok Salisbury differentials to assist performance in the Alps now that the engines could reach high revolutions safely and smoothly. One gets the impression that the works Sabre drivers found life hard work for little reward so were reluctant to stay with Reliant after one or two sorties, so further changes now saw Graham A. Warner of the Chequered Flag Garage driving 650 GUE with Peter Roberts and 649 GUE had Bobby Parkes at the helm as usual. 648 GUE was still not considered fit for action, but Graham P. Warner from Suffolk in his privately entered, two-headlight Sabre 6 (WGV 287), completed the team. Coincidentally, both Graham Warners had wives named Shirley. The cars were now looking quite impressive in sparkling white livery, sprouting numerous lights, louvres in the bonnets and substantial sump guards. They were performing well, too and becoming a force to be recognised — if not reckoned with. Their progress to Monte Carlo was uneventful until disaster struck the Parkes/Senior car when

The effects of a 70ft fall on a rally Sabre 6 — drivers escaped with only mild injuries.

Sabres In Rallying

a front studded tyre burst as Arthur Senior was negotiating a hairpin only 1½ hours from the finish. The Sabre crashed through a wall and dropped 70 feet on to the road below, which they should have reached by a rather longer route. The car was badly damaged, but it protected the crew from all but cuts and bruises due to its rigid chassis and strong bodywork, which absorbed impact rather than creasing as a steel monocoque might have done. All was not lost as Graham A. Warner finished his first ever rally 94th overall and 4th in class, while his namesake was 5th in class, so maintaining the excellent finishing record of the rally Sabres. Bobby Parkes was understandably pale and subdued after the rally, but was soon heard to ask "when is the next event?" There would never be another works entry in International rallies as the commercial standing of the Sabre did not justify further expenditure in competition. Reliant had demonstrated the strength, stamina and speed of their sporting product: they now had to refine it so that more people could be persuaded to buy it. Alex Griffiths acquired a works prepared Sabre 6 (660 XYB) which he continued to campaign privately during 1964/65 culminating in the 1965 Monte in which he did not finish.

Alex Griffiths watching his Sabre 6 being built with Arthur Rusling (right).

THE SCIMITAR AND ITS FOREBEARS

Sabre 6 chassis no. SS300123 used as a publicity car and now in Holland.

Shaun Bryne's immaculate Scimitar V6 Coupé pauses in the Cotswolds.

THE SCIMITAR AND ITS FOREBEARS

xiv

A lakeside view of an SE5a finished in Beaujolais Red.

Len Huff's SE6 custom painted in Caspian Blue with Trafalgar Blue band.

SUMMARY OF RALLY SABRE ACHIEVEMENTS

Event	Reg. No.	Driver/Co-Driver	No.	Result
Tulip Rally May 1962	15 CUE Sabre 4	Arthur Rusling Peter Easten	16	Retired
R.A.C. Rally November 1962	42 ENX Sabre 4	Bob Aston Gerry Cooper	78	34th place
	15 CUE Sabre 4	Jimmy Ray John Hopwood	27	38th place
	7 EUE Sabre 4	Tony Fisher John King	36	Retired rear axle
	6 EUE Sabre 4	Derrick Astle Peter Roberts	25	Retired
Monte Carlo Rally January 1963	6 EUE Sabre 4	Derrick Astle Peter Roberts	139	3rd in class
	7 EUE Sabre 4	Tony Fisher David Skeffington	172	92nd Hit church and damaged lights
	42 ENX Sabre 4	Jimmy Ray Mike Hughes	156	Retired
	342 ENX Regal 3-wheel	Cecil Sandford David Cooper		Press
Circuit of Ireland April 1963	42 ENX Sabre 4	Tony Fisher Ronald Crellin		3rd in class
Coup Des Alpes June 1963	648 GUE Sabre 6	Jimmy Ray Peter Roberts	1	Hit tree half way — retired
	650 GUE Sabre 6	Roger Clark Bob Aston	2	2nd in class
	649 GUE Sabre 6	Bobby Parkes Gerry Cooper	3	1st in class
Spa-Sofia-Liege August 1963	649 GUE Sabre 6	Bobby Parkes Arthur Senior	6	Hit wolf at 100kph — retired
	648 GUE Sabre 6	Raymond Baxter Douglas Wilson-Spratt	7	Hit bollard, left road — retired
	650 GUE Sabre 6	Robin Richards Alec Lobb	114	Crew fatigue — retired
R.A.C. Rally November 1963	649 GUE Sabre 6	Bobby Parkes Roy Dixon	16	3rd in unlimited GT class
	650 GUE Sabre 6	Raymond Baxter Ernest McMillen	18	Burst tyre, in ditch — retired
	42 ENX Sabre 4	Leslie Griffiths Stuart Turner	69	Private entry, 6th in class, 65th overall
	WGV 287 Sabre 6	Graham P. Warner John Spiers	176	Private entry — retired
Monte Carlo Rally January 1964	649 GUE Sabre 6	Bobby Parkes Arthur Senior	263	Fell 70ft 30 miles from finish — retired
	650 GUE Sabre 6	Graham A. Warner Peter Roberts	247	4th in class, 94th overall
	WGV 287 Sabre 6	Graham P. Warner John Spiers	43	Private entry 5th in class, 158th overall
Welsh Rally January 1964	648 GUE Sabre 6	Bobby Parkes Peter Roberts	12	2nd in class, 14th overall
	42 ENX Sabre 4	Alex Griffiths Stuart Turner	29	Private entry 1st in class, 13th overall
Monte Carlo Rally January 1965	660 XYB Sabre 6	Alex Griffiths Stuart Turner	99	Private entry — retired

Sabres In Rallying

The Competitions Department still had the lightweight car intended for the 1963 Le Mans race, but again its entry was refused due to over subscription by better known makes, so Arthur decided to let Bobby Parkes use it in hill climbs where he achieved many class wins by virtue of its quite shattering performance. This is illustrated by figures obtained by 'Autocar' magazine when they tested it in road trim and registered 867 HWD:

	876 HWD	**4.2 E-type**
mph	sec	sec
0-40	3.2	4.1
0-60	6.1	7.6
0-80	11.1	11.7
0-100	22.0	17.5
Standing ¼ mile	15.2	15.1

This car was fitted with a 4 speed ZF gearbox, as in the Sabre 4, to gain the benefit of its light weight and close ratios. Later it was fitted with a 5 speed ZF unit as found in the contemporary Alvis 3-litre models in order to gain a higher top speed for racing purposes. To improve its rear wheel adhesion, David Page was given a free hand to re-design the oft-maligned rear suspension to cure its maladies. He evolved a double wishbone independent system with fully adjustable links attached to extensions fabricated on to the rear of the chassis, to which the differential was now rigidly mounted. The wheel uprights were made from Rover 2000 components and outboard discs

Works Sprint Sabre 6 cornering hard — note flattened rear wheel arches.

retained. These modifications increased the rear track by 4in so the rear wheel arches were widened and flattened to accommodate the 6in Borrani wheels. To match this squat rear end the front track was also widened and a 4in strip let into the middle of the bonnet to balance the appearance of this now quite attractive vehicle. In this form it was loaned to Tony Marsh, the then Hill Climb Champion, for certain events as a publicity exercise and his ascent of Shelsley Walsh in 39 seconds drew much more favourable and astonished comment. Arthur Rusling forsook his ever faithful 15 CUE road car in favour of 876 HWD when it was retired from active competition for a couple of years. It was then sold to Robert Marsland who continued to use it for sprints and hill climbs where in other hands it still continues to appear, 23 years on.

The ex-works sprint car in new livery as raced by Robin Rew in the 1970's.

SABRES IN RALLYING

As we have seen, a few Sabres were campaigned privately in rallies alongside the works cars, but they were also raced privately, notably by the Sabre dealers Steering Wheel Garage and Argyle Motors in Birkenhead who bought one of the development Sabre 6s, (811 FUE), for such purposes. Graham Warner of the former concern originally campaigned a Sabre 4 in races (7947 WD) driven by Peter Swinger, before using the Sabre 6 (WGV 287) in rallies and races. He even managed to put the Sabre in the record books by lapping Snetterton circuit for 24 hours at an average speed of 70.18mph, assisted by Mike Watts and with the moral support of Arthur Rusling and Lai Parkes from Reliant, who came along out of enthusiasm for this attempt on the Commander's Cup. The car (WGT 889) was absolutely standard from the showroom, with only iodine headlamps and harder brake linings fitted to combat the continuous high speed driving conditions.

These additional competition activities were still not sufficient to induce sales of the cars to the public and it was abundantly clear from press comment alone that priority must be given to appearance and comfort if Reliant hoped to succeed in the Grand Touring market they were now aiming at with the Sabre 6. The Tamworth concern was by tradition an engineering company and had no stylists within their ranks and they were soldiering on with a bodyshape originally chosen by the Israelis, ostensibly for the US market. It was obvious, even to Ray Wiggin, that they would now have to look outside the company for a more attractive shape with which to adorn their proven mechanicals.

The record-breaking standard Sabre 6 having a pit stop at Snetterton.

7 EUE awaiting restoration by Ken Trickett.

The late Roger Valler competing in the autotest at Blenheim Palace during the 1982 'Golden 50' rally, navigated by Geoff Cooper.

Sabres In Rallying

Roger Heron using the ex-Roger Clark car on an autotest.

Robin Rew ascending Barbon Hill Climb, having re-built 648 GUE.

John Valler in full flight on the 1984 Coronation Rally on the Eppynt.

The Ogle connection

Q. What is a Grand Touring car?

A. It's a car like the SCIMITAR GT

Q. *And what's a Scimitar GT?*		**A.**	It's a 120-m.p.h. saloon with seats for three (four if necessary) club armchair comfort, train-like roadholding and comfort and performance to spare.
Q. *Fabulously expensive?*		**A.**	Not really, it just looks that way. The Reliant Motor Company feel that as they can sell it for less than £1,300 and still make a living—it's being sold for less than £1,300.
Q. *Ah, but what about the extras— they push the price up don't they?*		**A.**	If by extras you mean things like a three-carburettor engine conversion, full heating and demisting equipment, windshield washers, wire wheels, Cinturato tyres, sumptuous seating, full instrumentation and the rest— they are all included in the price. If you want an extra touch of luxury, of course, the Scimitar can be supplied with an electrically-operated sliding roof, de Normanville overdrive, and a few other bits and pieces.
Q. *What about servicing after sales?*		**A.**	There's a Reliant dealer in your neighbourhood. Have a word with him now, or write direct to Reliant. (For real kick-in-the-back acceleration, sort-the-men-from-the-boys motoring, with just a trace of luxury, there's still the Sabre Six sports and GT range at less than £1,100).

Scimitar GT and Sabre Six engineered by:

THE RELIANT MOTOR COMPANY LIMITED,
Tamworth, Staffordshire, England.

CHAPTER 4

The Ogle connection

UP TO THIS point the introduction and progress of Reliant's sporting cars had been influenced largely by persons and organisations outside the company itself. They did not undertake the Sabra project with the intention of producing it in the UK, let alone selling it here as well. Neither did they plan to enter international competition and form a separate department to control this activity. It was now time to grasp the nettle firmly and try and make a commercial success out of all the effort and limited funds expended on the Sabre. Ray Wiggin's enthusiasm for this type of car had been instrumental in sanctioning its continued development within fairly tight limits. He often had to battle against Tom Williams whose heart was firmly in the economy range, which after all was the really profitable part of the company and to everyone's amazement showed no signs of flagging. Ray Wiggin now had to justify his faith in the concept of sports car production to retain credibility with his superiors as well as the workforce, some of whom were sceptical of its worth. Everyone was aware that the Sabre was not achieving anything like the sales anticipated and some models stayed in the showroom as long as two years after production finished in 1964, but it was right there in the showroom that the Sabre largely failed before many potential customers ever went as far as sampling the car on the road. Reliant were not equipped to style a world class sports or Grand Touring car in-house, so they were forced to observe other stylists' work for inspiration, and what better place to survey their efforts than the annual Motor Show?

The Italian coachbuilders were way beyond Reliant's reach financially and in the early 1960s the only British car styling concern, then in its infancy, was Ogle Design whose first automotive application was announced in 1959. Four years later they exhibited their third car styling exercise at the 1962 Motor Show based on the Daimler SP250 (nee Dart) chassis. The Daimler had many parallels with the Sabre since, except for its V8 power unit, it featured a cruciform ladder chassis with Triumph-based front suspension and a controversial, some would say ugly, fibreglass body, which hindered its sales despite its undoubted dynamic qualities. Ogle's fixed head version, called the SX250, caught Ray Wiggin's eye and this chance observation led to a milestone in the history of Reliant as well as Ogle Design.

Coincidentally, Ogle had been involved in car design for about the same time as Reliant had been producing four-wheeled cars, but as a company Ogle was far younger, having been founded in 1954 by David Ogle, a pilot in the Fleet Air Arm during the Second World War. After demobilisation he took a course in design at the Central School of Arts and Craft in London, then joined Murphy Radio as a designer. Although Murphy had some advanced and successful ideas about design, Ogle really wanted to be independent, so he set himself

The Ogle-bodied Daimler SX250 at the 1962 Motor Show which attracted Ray Wiggin's attention.

up as a design consultant before leaving Murphy in 1954. Ironically, his first major account customer was Murphy's rival in the radio business, Bush Radio, for whom he designed two extremely successful products, the TR82 Radio and the SRP31D record player.

Ogle's business grew slowly and he formed his first company, David Ogle Associates in 1959, necessitating a move from an office in his house to premises in Stevenage new town, north of London. Here David was assisted by a secretary and four designers, one of whom was Tom Karen, the present Managing Director of Ogle Design. The other three all went on to found their own successful design studios. Karen was born in Vienna in 1926 and after studying engineering at Loughborough College gained extensive design experience in the aircraft industry from 1945-55 when he switched to cars at the Ford Styling Department for four years before joining Ogle. Tom Karen recalls that Ogle had a gift for producing advanced designs which were nevertheless not regarded as odd by the average man and so had immediate sales appeal. It was a philosophy which Raymond Loewy, consultant to Studebaker and Rootes, called MAYA — Most Advanced Yet Acceptable. Ogle also had a flair for designing forms that were nice to handle and he was always concerned with the need for easy tooling and simplicity of manufacture. Ogle was keen to become involved in car design and his first study in 1959 was based on the Riley 1.5, which in its day was quite a competitive sporting saloon made by BMC, but blessed with a rather staid body shape. Initial impressions of the Ogle 1.5 are very reminiscent of the delightful Alfa Romeo Guilietta Sprint, but the 'grinning' grille and tail fins are less attractive to this writer's eyes. Ogle did not restrict his design changes to merely attaching a new fibreglass body to the BMC floorpan and mechanicals, but added a tubular chassis extension to the rear of this platform to accommodate a coil spring and trailing arm rear suspension system in place of the original semi-elliptic leaf springs. Despite being no less than 7in lower than the parent car, four people could still fit into the all-leather seats and the shallow boot could house a set of golf clubs alongside the fuel filler fitted inside this compartment (a feature also shared by the Giulietta Sprint). As a result of weighing some 90lb less than the steel bodied Riley saloon, plus the adoption of 13in wheels instead of the 14in variety, the acceleration was much more lively. For example, 50-70mph in top gear came down from 22.4sec to 17.0sec and the top speed rose by 5mph. Standing start acceleration was still rather leisurely by today's standards, since it took 20sec to reach 60mph. Looking at the car it would certainly be difficult to detect its origins, and the only original external body part utilised was in fact the windscreen, fitted at a different angle of rake.

Ogle's first car body design based on the Riley 1.5 with a similar roofline to the Alfa Romeo Giulietta Sprint.

Only eight of these rare models were produced and the transition from design to actual small scale production necessitated a move to larger premises at Birds Hill in Letchworth, Herts, where Ogle Design are still based, employing some of the original model makers to this day. Simultaneously, a new company, David Ogle Ltd, was set up and work began in 1960 on the next automotive project based on the recently introduced Mini. The principles used in the Ogle 1.5 were again featured in the new Ogle Mini (SX1000), consisting of a fibreglass bodyshell bonded onto the base frame of the production car, but no modifications were deemed necessary to the suspension in this case, which is hardly surprising. Again a marked reduction in overall height was achieved, by 6in this time, but the total length and width were increased 12in and 2½in respectively. This limited accommodation to two persons in luxury, plus luggage, and a 13½ gallon fuel tank, which permitted well over 400 miles of non-stop motoring if required. Any of the Mini engines could be fitted, and the improved drag figures (around 8% better) gave the Cooper-engined versions a top speed approaching 100mph. Acceleration was barely altered since the overall weight and gearing were unchanged this time. From the side view, a distinct similarity of line is very evident with the Ogle 1.5, particularly in the shape of the door and side windows and the rather high waistline forced on the design by the relatively tall mechanical components of the parent vehicle. About 66

The Ogle SX 1000 based on the Mini floorpan.

The Ogle Connection

Ogle Minis were made at Letchworth and today they are becoming sought after as they were probably the best looking and most professionally made Mini specials ever. A fleeting re-appearance of this model, called the Fletcher GT, was exhibited at the 1963 Racing Car Show, but few were actually made. Tragically, David Ogle met his death in an Ogle Mini on his way to Brands Hatch for a race meeting and his partner in the company, John Ogier, assumed command as Chairman, inviting Tom Karen to become Managing Director. This upheaval occurred in 1962 when the company were in the middle of the next Ogle design commissioned by a cosmetics firm based on the Daimler SP250 sports car chassis. Clearly, from the eventual bodyshape David Ogle had been influential in the design of the resulting Ogle SX250, even though it was left to his able successors to finalise the car, ready for the 1962 Motor Show in London. One of these was Carl Olsen, who had been trained in the Pratt Institute in New York and later worked for General Motors in Detroit before joining Bernadotte & Bjorne Design of Denmark, his home country.

Profile of one of the two Ogle Daimlers produced.

Ogle Daimler being fabricated at Ogle Design (top & bottom).

The Ogle Connection

Although far more elegant than the two predecessors, the SX250 had the characteristic high waistline and the window profiles and roofline bear a distinct family resemblance to the Riley and Mini based forerunners. In addition, longer bonnet and boot proportions were now possible due to the extended wheelbase, with clean front and rear aspects which are still pleasing 20 years on. Attractive though Ray Wiggin found this new shape it was not for sale, so to speak, and destined to be a possible new Daimler model.

However, Reliant were on the point of finalising the design of their first four-wheeled passenger car, the FW4 to be later known as the Rebel, for the UK market. The three-wheelers up to that time had been styled, for want of a better word, in-house, but their new model was now going to face direct competition from the large mass-producers and must therefore attract customers by its appearance as well as economy. While BMC and Standard-Triumph could afford to use Italian consultants such as Pininfarina and Michelotti respectively to style their new models, a young British design house like Ogle was perhaps just the tonic Reliant needed to re-shape their future products. Wiggin was thus quick to engage Ogle Design for the FW4 saloon and estate as well as the TW9 three-wheeler commercial vehicles, to be later known as the Ant and a familiar sight in many council fleets' town work. Ogle were naturally keen to accept their new business and the results were obviously welcomed by Reliant, since all subsequent revisions to the economy range have been styled by the Letchworth company.

Wooden facia of Daimler SX 250.

Increasing pressure from all quarters was applied to Ray Wiggin to refine and re-shape the ailing Sabre 6 which, despite its competition achievements, was just not selling. Discreet enquiries were made through the trade as to the destiny of the SX250 which had attracted Wiggin so much on first sight. Fortunately for Reliant, the initial contract for six Ogle Daimlers resulted in only two being built and it seemed Ogle had a redundant design on their hands looking for a chassis. Comparisons between chassis dimensions revealed that the wheelbase of the Daimler was only 2in longer than that of the Sabre, while they shared identical front track, and the rear track of the Reliant was actually 1½in wider. The possibility of re-mounting the new Ogle body on the Sabre chassis seemed very real to both concerns and the moulds were transported to the Development Department at Two Gates for Ken Wood and his team to build a car on that basis. Detail changes were made to almost every area of the SX250 body to enable a satisfactory 2+2 Grand Touring car. Firstly, the rear seat 'was a joke' as Ken put it, offering absolutely no leg room, so this had to be moved back about 6in, rendering it necessary to extend the roofline backwards to provide minimal headroom. In order to reach these seats they found it necessary to increase the length of the doors by 5in. The wheelbase of the Sabre chassis was extended by 2in to match that of the Daimler, but the combination of the alterations made so far gave the impression of the rear axle having been moved forward, as the gap between the rear edge of the door and the front of the wheel arch was now reduced. The position of the

Reliant Scimitar Coupé featuring subtle modifications on the original Daimler model.

rear axle then gave the appearance of more overhang than Ogle intended, but Ken Wood's team rounded off the rear wheel arch to match the front ones, which helped to restore the balance. More rounded front and rear bumpers were adapted from the front item of the Ford Classic Capri, which was also the source of the windscreen. Smoothing the contours was extended to the headlamp area where the Perspex covered square apertures were shaped around the twin circular head-light bezels of the Triumph 2000. These important modifications did nothing to detract from the elegance of the Ogle concept and if anything produced a more co-ordinated result, so that the Reliant Board were in no doubt about the wisdom of proceeding with this project, to be coded SE4.

It was now the turn of the chassis engineers under David Page to cater for the extra 2cwt of bodywork arising from the new design. The Sabre 6 chassis had proved itself capable of handling more power from its rallying activities, but it was felt that the new model, intended as a touring car, would require softer springing than the more sporting Sabre. In conjunction with Aeon Rubber technicians, Reliant development engineers fitted out a fleet of Sabre 6s with a range of non-standard suspension units incorporating Aeon Rubber assist-springs at the rear to give some indication of the best combination to be used on the SE4. Meanwhile another group of engineers were concentrating on extracting more power from the venerable 2,553cc Ford engine so that the new car could achieve a top speed in the region of 120mph with acceleration to match. Preliminary tests were made with an engine fitted with three SU carburettors, which raised the power output to 120bhp. When tested at MIRA with this power unit, the prototype lapped the test track at 110-115mph and over a period of six months of road use produced a comparatively good fuel consumption figure of 22/26mpg. A second prototype, registered AUE 38B as an Ogle GT, was produced with the engine

Twin headlights with sculptured bezels similar to Triumph 2000 units.

moved forward 6in in the chassis to equalise weight distribution when the car was laden and also permitting slightly more room for the front passengers. This was the final specification adopted and the Sabre 6 braking was utilised unchanged as it had proved perfectly adequate for competition use. The front suspension vertical links were changed from the TR4 pattern to a slightly different, but stronger type as fitted to the SP250 from whence the body design had appeared. Surprisingly the disc-braked rear axle from that model was not incorporated, in view of the similar performance and weight of the two cars.

Within 18 months of the plan being initiated the new car, christened the Scimitar GT, was ready for the 1964 Earls Court Motor Show. Internally the new SE4 was very well finished with a mock-wood facia, leather-covered steering wheel, gear and door controls and vinyl seats with cloth inlays for added comfort and grip. The new Ogle designed Rebel appeared for the first time at the same Motor Show and the Reliant stand was certainly one of the busiest in the whole exhibition, as this writer well remembers. The new Scimitar immediately won praise for its elegant lines and the promised qualities in performance, comfort and handling unobtainable at double the asking price of £1,292. That promise was yet to be fulfilled, as the ever interested journalist Edward Eves discovered when he drove one of the first production models to Monza and back. The deficiencies of the old Sabre rear suspension were still present and emphasised now that the spring rates had been softened, and Eves was convinced that urgent attention to this system was imperative if the Scimitar was ever to become accepted as a worthy Grand Touring car, which it was capable of being with such long-legged performance and a huge 21 gallon fuel tank permitting up to 500 miles of non-stop motoring.

Front and rear coil spring suspensions very similar to Sabre 6 predecessor.

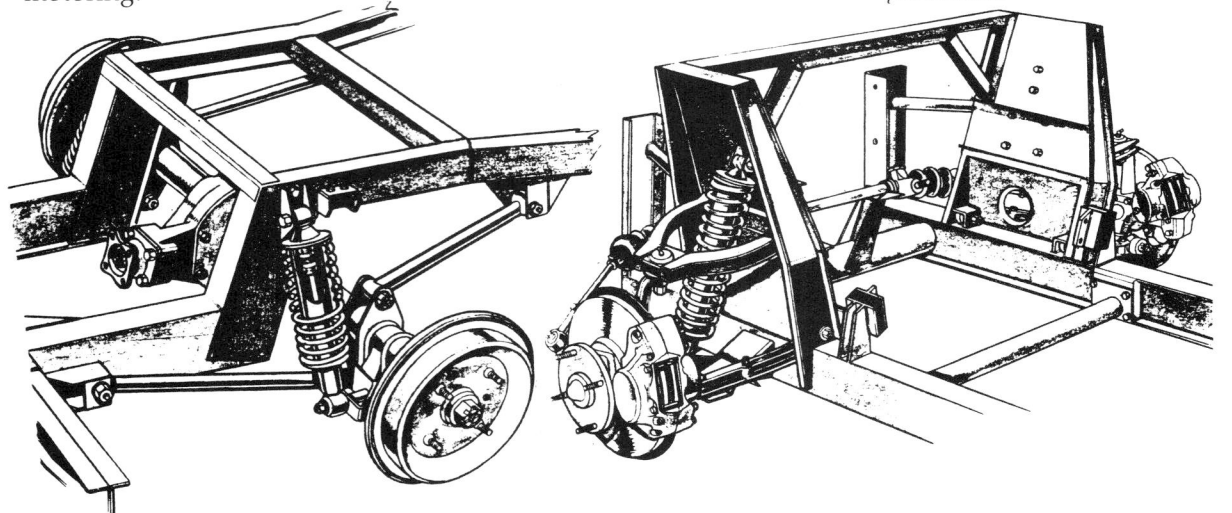

The Ogle Connection

Other motoring scribes reported the same reservations while applauding the high speed capabilities of the new Scimitar. For instance, the 'Autocar' road test said "by making full use of the gears, this car's pace on country roads can result in surprisingly rapid average speeds with comfort, an easy cruising speed being about 90mph, and on motorways one can bowl along at up to 105mph with very little mechanical fuss. Steering, by rack and pinion, is light and precise, but with considerable road reaction fed back to the leather covered steering wheel. The rear suspension, however, seems to need firmer transverse location, since there is an initial sideways lurch as the Watt linkage rubbers take up the load whenever a change of direction is made. Once the axle has assumed its new position, control becomes safe and predictable."

Edward Eves conveyed his concern about the rear suspension to Ray Wiggin, together with a low cost solution to the problem in his view. This involved turning the top leading arm on each side of the car through 180° so that they became the upper arms of parallel trailing links. Wiggin accepted this suggestion and within a week a modified car was ready. The modification included a small Watt linkage attached to the differential housing to afford accurate sideways location for the axle, as opposed to a lateral panhard rod used by Aston Martin among others. A weekend on the Continent testing this new system satisfied Eves that the ride and handling were transformed. David Page went one stage further by fitting an independent wishbone rear suspension to one of the works fleet, chassis no. 7, along the lines already used on the racing Sabre, 876 HWD. However, this system demands a more rigid chassis construction than a live axle and this manifested itself by the rear window becoming dislodged on very rough roads due to body flexing. This problem, allied to the extra weight and considerable cost, rendered it a very fascinating non-starter, and the twin trailing arm arrangement was adopted after 59 cars had been produced.

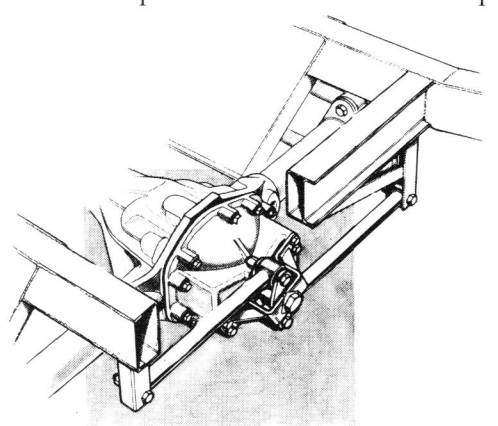

Modified rear axle location using a lateral Watts linkage and twin trailing arms markedly improved handling.

Production now rose to 15 cars a week, most of which were equipped with the Ford four speed gearbox with Laycock overdrive, but the ZF four speed box originally used on the Sabre 4 was offered as an option combined with a 3.58:1 axle to ratio as opposed to the standard 3.88:1 gearing. It seems most likely that Reliant had several of these units left in store and hoped that offering it as a sporting alternative would reduce their stocks of these rather expensive assemblies. Nowadays SE4s fitted with this gearbox are sought after for the purpose of obtaining the ZF product for transplant into Sabre 6s or Lotus Elites. The only other options offered for this well equipped GT car were a radio, seat belts and a manual or electric sliding sunroof, while the wire wheels were standard, setting off the smooth body contours most effectively. The Scimitar GT, or Coupé as it is now generally known, was at last a serious contender in the

Mock wood facia of Straight Six Scimitar Coupé with well placed instruments.

The Ogle Connection

sporting car market against such respected rivals as the Austin Healey 3000 and the Sunbeam Tiger, both in price and performance as the following road test figures reveal:

	Scimitar GT	Austin Healey 3000 Mk III	Sunbeam Tiger
Capacity (cc)	2,553	2,912	4,200
Power (bhp)	116	150	141
Max speed (mph)	117	122	116
0-60mph (secs)	10.1	9.8	9.4
Standing ¼ mile (secs)	17.9	17.0	17.4
mpg (touring)	26.9	24.5	21.7
Weight (cwt)	21.2	23.0	23.1
Price (£)	1,352	1,166	1,446

Scimitar Coupé production line at Two Gates factory.

One particular example of Reliant's new Grand Tourer was destined to attain world-wide fame as a result of a commission given to Ogle by Triplex Safety Glass to explore the increased use of glass in car bodywork style and construction, now that face level ventilation was so effective in modern cars. Ogle started work in January 1965 on the design and construction of a running prototype. Though they would have preferred to design a completely new car, it was felt that the cost would not have been justified, so it was decided to take an existing design of their own, the Scimitar GT, and re-design it from the waist upwards.

Among the various drawings that Ogle put forward was the estate car version, representing an entirely original GT concept. This had the merits of offering, on a small car, a full four seater passenger compartment for the study of solar energy versus ventilation problems appropriate to a family-sized saloon. It avoided the optical drawbacks of the excessive fast back rake angles, common to many GT specials and enabled maximum rear vision to be used with full-depth demisting, but only modest electrical consumption. The Triplex laboratory at Holly Grange designed glazing sections to give minimum pillar widths and carried out the adhesive glazing on the finished car.

Ogle GTS (Glazing Test Special) in profile.

Additional features in the specification included a wire-heated windscreen, using crimped wires to eliminate light scatter. This idea was later used in rally cars in events carried out in sub-zero temperatures and has only just crept into the optional extra list on Ford models in this country. Ogle incorporated a structural roll-bar to give protection and confidence to those who might be nervous of an all glass roof from a structural aspect. An alternator was used to take care of the additional electrical load imposed by the heated front and rear screens while Sundym heat-absorbing glass was used in all panels to control solar heat problems.

This unique vehicle, known as the Ogle GTS (Glazing Test Special) was introduced to the press at the Europa Hotel on 15th October immediately before the annual Motor Show at Earls Court where it appeared, naturally enough, on the Ogle stand. Here it was closely examined by many of the captains of the motor industry as well as such notable personalities as Lord Snowdon and Nubar Gulbenkian who discussed the use of similar techniques in his next limousine. Immediately after the London show the car was driven to Turin for the motor show there, in the heart of the prototype coachbuilding centre of the world, where it was much admired by the Italian designers.

Extensive use of glass evident from this angle.

Soon after its return to this country, His Royal Highness the Duke of Edinburgh acquired the car, cleverly registered 66 OGLE, from Triplex for his personal use and thus commenced a 20 year association between the Royal Family and Reliant motor cars. The Duke had previously owned Alvis and Lagonda convertibles and his choice of the Ogle GTS did much to enhance the reputation of the Scimitar, on which it was recognisably developed. Subsequently, Triplex re-purchased the car from the Duke after some 18 months of regular use and exhibited it at various shows and motor sport events. For example it was course car at the 1969 British Grand Prix at Brands Hatch. A fitting retirement for this famous car came about in 1973 when Triplex handed their mobile test-bed over to Lord Montague on permanent loan for exhibition in the newly opened National Motor Museum at Beaulieu, where it can be seen on those days when it is not out on display at Classic Car shows.

Ogle GTS being handed over to Lord Montague (far right) at Beaulieu by Ray Wiggin and Tom Karen (by driver's door).

The Ogle Connection

Prince Philip leaving the Ogle GTS during his period of ownership.

Substantial built-in roof rack and large tailgate are advanced features.

Two years after the introduction of the new Scimitar GT, by which time 297 examples had left Tamworth, Ford ceased production of the straight six Zephyr/Zodiac range of cars from which Reliant had borrowed the power unit. The radical Mk IV range of large Ford saloons arrived, now powered by 3-litre V6 engines and Reliant had little option but to modify the Scimitar where necessary to accommodate this more compact, as well as more powerful, unit. At this point Reliant consulted John Crosthwaite, who had previously been a chassis designer for BRM, about improving the suspension of the Scimitar still further, in view of the increased power now envisaged. The Scimitar had always felt as if it was on tip-toe in severe cornering situations, as a result of the rather high roll-centre of the front suspension. This was the first area that Crosthwaite attacked, by lowering the mounting points of the upper and lower wishbone inner pivots on the chassis, thereby lowering the roll-centre from 6.5in to 2.5in from the ground. It was now necessary to fit an anti-roll bar between the front suspension to limit the roll angles, but the new layout virtually eliminated front tyre scrub during suspension movement. At the rear of the chassis he re-located the front pivots of the trailing arms outwards, so that the arms were now parallel with the main chassis rails, which helped to reduce roll-steer effects caused by the splayed arrangement imposed by the need to use up the stocks of angled trailing arms left over from Sabre production. John Crosthwaite now found it was possible to increase the rear wheel movement by 3in, particularly in rebound, without detrimental side

Ford V6 engine sits well back in the substantial Scimitar chassis.

effects. This he did, by lengthening the rods of the shock absorbers, which now acted as restrictors on total wheel movement downwards in place of the webbing straps used for this purpose on the earlier cars. The shorter V6 engine was sited further back in the chassis than its predecessor, resulting in a 50:50 weight distribution when laden, contributing to the excellent handling of the V6 Scimitar Coupés, as they became known. The new model, coded SE4a, was virtually indistinguishable from the SE4 externally, apart from a 3-litre badge discreetly placed on the rear body panel and a re-shaping of the front valence below the front bumper to accommodate the new anti-roll bar. An additional crossmember in the chassis strengthened that area. Also hidden from view were stronger steel reinforcements round the doors to provide a secure anchorage for new burst-proof locks. Inside the new car an all black theme replaced the part wood and part cloth decor of the SE4, with a basket-weave effect on the seats to break up the rather plain appearance. New face-level air outlets appeared on the dashboard in line with the latest developments in ventilation pioneered by the Ford Cortina, but no corresponding outlets were provided except for the opening rear quarter-lights. Rear seat accommodation was slightly increased by re-shaping the backrest, but it was still only possible to carry two pre-teenage children in that area.

The all-black vinyl trim of the 3-litre Scimitar Coupé. Note the air vents.

The disc steel wheels were far less attractive than the earlier wire variety.

Wire wheels were now considered too expensive, even as an optional extra, as was the ZF gearbox and steel wheels with chrome embellishers and the Zodiac Mk IV gearbox were the standard fitments, although overdrive was an option. Apart from the previous optional extras of a radio and manual or electric sliding sunroof, a heated rear screen was now offered, made of laminated glass with the heating elements between the two glass layers, as first seen on the Ogle GTS. Clearly all the modifications transformed the Scimitar, as such eminent motoring personalities as Stirling Moss and John Bolster reported after trying the revised model. Stirling considered the car "now qualifies for the classic definition of a grand touring car — one which permits driver and passenger and their luggage to cover long distances on European high speed roads in complete comfort. It looks good, it is handsomely finished and carefully thought out." John Bolster of 'Autosport' found "the Scimitar likes to go fast. It likes long journeys on open roads, but is now happy to be flung round sharp corners, the rear suspension behaving beautifully. Generally,

The V6 engine was virtually buried under suppression sheild; note twin 6-volt batteries.

there is slight understeer and the machine is very stable in consequence. On good roads, the maximum speed of well over 120mph may be enjoyed without any drama, sidewinds having little effect". Bill Boddy, Editor of 'Motor Sport' was still not over enamoured by the latest Reliant GT, however, and he summed up the SE4a by concluding that "for those who want a not-too-expensive, very high peformance GT-type car, the 3-litre Reliant Scimitar has much in its favour. For me, however, it is marred by the nasty gear change, badly-placed minor controls, uncomfortable seats, far too lively ride over secondary roads and a cramped interior with the window winders tending to jab the driver; the intrusion of fumes, heat and the sense of being in a 'components' car also putting me off." This just goes to prove that Reliant could not please everyone, but the ever loyal Edward Eves now acquired a Coupé as his 'Autocar' staff car and even entered it in the 1969 Austrian Journalists Rally. He had to enter his car in the Unlimited Sports Prototype category as the Scimitar had not been homologated, but it still won the class when most of the opposition retired (shades of the 1963 Alpine Rally when the Sabres were 1st and 2nd in their class). During a period of two years driving, Eves considered it ideal for fast journeys across the Continent on reporting missions and achieved an overall fuel consumption of 24.6mpg. He even had the misfortune to demonstrate the safe construction of his car when he was involved in a sandwich collision on the M1. Both front and rear ends suffered extensive crumpling of the fibreglass bodywork and chassis outriggers, but the passenger compartment was totally undamaged, easily fulfilling the requirements of modern, obligatory crumple zones.

The Scimitar now began to sell in encouraging numbers, justifying at last all the hard work and investment put into the project by Reliant over six years. Such progress was suddenly thwarted in 1967 when the Arab-Israeli Seven Day War in the Sinai Desert threatened petrol supplies to the West, causing an immediate price rise which rendered large-engined cars less desirable overnight. Reliant were able to respond by offering the 2.5-litre V6 engine based on the same cylinder block as an alternative model (known as the SE4c) costing about £120 less. Naturally the performance of the car was affected to the extent that the top speed was down by 10mph and it took three seconds longer to reach 60mph from standstill. However, the fuel consumption was only improved by around 1mpg overall and the SE4c was even thirstier than the 3-litre car over 80mph. Further small improvements were made to the interior of the 3-litre car simultaneously to try and maintain sales of the larger engined car, now termed the SE4b. The following 'Motor' road test results show how the two Scimitars compared with their competitors:

	Scimitar GT 3-litre	**MGC GT**	**Scimitar 2.5-litre**	**Triumph TR5**
Capacity (cc)	2,994	2,912	2,495	2,500
Power (bhp)	144	145	119	142
Max speed (mph)	120.9	120	111	117
0-60mph (secs)	9.4	10.0	12.3	8.1
mpg (overall)	19.3	19.3	21.7	19.9
Weight (cwt)	21.6	22.2	21	20.4
Price (£)	1,577	1,337	1,450	1,305

The untidy array of rear lights common to the Hillman Imp among others.

The only other change to the specification of both models occurred in August 1968, when quite unannounced the front suspension was changed from the original Daimler SP250 set-up using brass bushes in the outer ends of the lower front wishbones to the latest Triumph TR6 type which employed sturdier vertical links with corresponding trunnions, now linked to the wishbone with maintenance free nylon bushes. This coincided with the introduction of the GTE, which like all subsequent Scimitars has retained basically the same IFS system. In the case of the Coupé the 5in × 15in steel wheels had to be slightly modified to accommodate the revised suspension links. These wheels can be identified by radial slots near the rim normally hidden by the garish chrome embellishers so popular at the time. The V6-engined Coupés always lacked the distinctive appearance of the straight Six forebears following the replacement of the wire wheels by the cheaper steel variety. Many subsequent owners in recent years have fitted more attractive, wider alloy wheels effecting dramatic improvements to both handling and looks of these intrinsically attractive cars.

Apart from the wheels it is difficult to tell the difference between early and later cars.

For reasons which will be revealed in the next chapter the Scimitar Coupé ceased production in 1970 after 590 3-litre and 117 2.5-litre models had been made over a period of four years. However an attempt was made by John Crosthwaite in conjunction with the body development team to produce an updated version of the Coupé in 1970. This featured front and rear bodywork changes to an old demonstration car, ARF 109D, along the lines of the GTE which had been introduced in 1968 together with chassis modifications borrowed from the later model too. Only one of these hybrids was officially produced, but Reg Mottram, who actually carried out the fibreglass work on the car admitted that at least one other Coupé received the same bodywork alterations and was registered JBF 653C.

The Coupé/GTE hybrid showing the GTE front grafted onto the Coupé body and the flared wheel arches to accommodate wider track axles.

Grand Touring Estate

Scimitar offers the impossible

Up front: bred like a racehorse. 0-60 in 8.6 seconds. Takes the motorway at a cantering 70 with 50-plus in reserve.

At the back: space for a cartload – anything from golf bags to Glyndebourne hampers. 19 cubic feet with all four seats up; 27 cubic feet with one back seat down; 36 cubic feet with them both down.

In between: comfort for four adults. The taut, road-hugging ride that only a thoroughbred Grand Tourer will give.

An impossible combination? Test drive it. That's all we ask.

To: Marketing Services, Reliant Motor Company Ltd., Tamworth, Staffs, B77 1HN.
☐ Please send me more details about the Scimitar GTE.
☐ Please arrange a road test.   ☐ If under 18 tick here.

Name

Address

Present Car

2294104

Scimitar GTE
HIGH PERFORMANCE ESTATE

CHAPTER 5

Grand Touring Estate

IN THE SCIMITAR Coupé, Reliant had a car with an elegant body, good performance and handling with a reasonable ride, but the market was very limited by its lack of four full-sized seats. One adult could sit crossways in the rear seat, but there was insufficient room for two teenage children without inviting vociferous complaints. Ray Wiggin knew that they really needed a four seater model to take full advantage of the potential built into the overall design. As early as 1966 Reliant were working hard on the possibilities of such an expanded model and it was then that John Crosthwaite became full-time Chief Engineer in charge of the project. It might have seemed logical to develop the Triplex GTS as a replacement model, but that car still had little or no rear seat space and lengthening the wheelbase would only make it more like an estate car than ever. Also on the stocks was a larger engined V8 version of the Scimitar Coupé, probably Chrysler powered, but as we have seen the Middle East crisis killed the market for larger engined cars, so the proposed SE3 never saw the light of day and the smaller brother with a 2.5-litre V6 was introduced instead.

Ray Wiggin had naturally discussed various ideas about body design with Tom Karen of Ogle, with whom Reliant had a styling agreement. For two years, however, no real progress was made in this direction and once again the stimulation for new thoughts came from a motor show, this time the 1967 Earls Court exhibition. Both men were very impressed with the packaging concept of the four seater V12 Lamborghini Espada, on show for the first time, but it was far too long and out of proportion due to the need to accommodate such a vast engine. Ray considered the one-off Zagato-bodied Rover 2000, called the TCZ, had a most admirable combination of styling and compactness, but was not quite large enough to fit in four

Zagato-bodied Rover TCZ which inspired Ray Wiggin when looking for a replacement for the Scimitar Coupé.

people. It appeared that the design would lend itself to providing more rear headroom than the Scimitar Coupé and with these thoughts in mind Tom Karen returned to Letchworth to attempt a blending operation of the various facets of the designs which had attracted them. Within a matter of days Tom had produced a mock-up of his ideas on a theme which stemmed back to some work he had done earlier on a design for an Anadol estate car. Initial work on investigating the possibilities of a more spacious Scimitar involved extending the glazed cabin area or 'Greenhouse', as Karen described it. This procedure ran into difficulties when trying to achieve a fast-back line with adequate headroom as the result began to look like a sort of Escort estate car due to the large areas of glass behind the 'B' pillar. Introducing extra pillars in this expanse of glass as on the proposed Anadol estate helped, but it was the rising rear wing line of that design which gave Karen the notion of extending that line upwards to the rear of the bodywork to produce a revolutionary wedge-like profile. This gave the impression that the rear wheels were larger than the front ones, creating a more sporting appearance. It was from this inspired experiment that the now well known GTE shape first evolved.

Proposed Anadol estate designed by Ogle which influenced the GTE shape.

GRAND TOURING ESTATE

The mock-up, which was presented to Wiggin when he visited Ogle Design soon after the meeting at the 1967 Motor Show, had a division down its centre line which featured the extended 'Greenhouse' plan for the Coupé on one side, while the rising waistline derived from the proposed Anadol estate was incorporated on the other side. In this instance, however, the roofline fell gently culminating in a slight up-turn or 'kick' before the sharply inclined opening rear window, which extended down well below the final level of the tapering side window. The shape of these side glasses also helped to balance the relatively shallow depth of the door windows, giving the impression of a lower waistline and deeper glass area at that point. The aspect which gave Tom Karen particular satisfaction was the manner in which the sculptured rear flanks of the body gave the required effect of 'tumblehome' to the rear of the car yet retaining straight glass at the side and door windows, set nearly vertically. Karen feared that such a dramatic shape might frighten Wiggin off his exciting new concept, since previous Reliant models had featured conservative styling. Much to his amazement, and relief, his fears were unnecessary, for when Ray had taken one look at the mock-up composed of netting, paper and cardboard glued

Hastily prepared mock-up of GTE outline on extended Coupé bodyshell which Ray Wiggin immediately approved.

together he exclaimed "that's it, let's go". He returned to Tamworth intent on persuading his colleagues on the Reliant Board to examine the Ogle Design team's efforts without delay. Before the ten day Motor Show, from whence the initiative sprang, had ended, the Reliant Board gave Karen the go-ahead for the bodywork of the Scimitar Coupé replacement, to become known as the GTE (Grand Touring Estate).

Curiously, the biggest headache in perfecting the new GTE shape was not concerned with the revolutionary rear end, but the frontal aspect. In an attempt to up-date the looks of the Scimitar Coupé front panel, the first prototype featured four oblong head-lamps in a full-width squared-off open grille. This was very mundane in appearance and after attempts to 'get it right' they reverted to a slightly flattened version of the Coupé front with less pronounced sculptured contours round the four circular headlamps.

The pace with which the whole design was then transformed from a crude mock-up to a production possibility was a tribute to the intense work of a small group of experts working directly under John Crosthwaite, Reliant's Chief Engineer of Vehicles. The various individuals involved in the development of the Scimitar and their responsibilities are shown below:

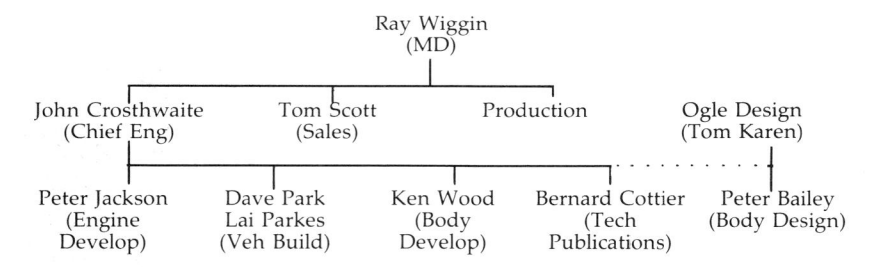

```
                        Ray Wiggin
                          (MD)
         ┌─────────────┬───┴─────┬──────────────┐
   John Crosthwaite  Tom Scott  Production  Ogle Design
   (Chief Eng)      (Sales)                  (Tom Karen)
         │             │           │              │
   Peter Jackson   Dave Park   Ken Wood    Bernard Cottier   Peter Bailey
   (Engine        Lai Parkes   (Body         (Tech           (Body Design)
   Develop)       (Veh Build)  Develop)      Publications)
```

Peter Bailey was fundamental in transforming Ogle's mock-up of the GTE shape into drawings from which pattern makers in Ken Wood's department could make moulds. Certain body parts from the Coupé, such as windscreen, door shells and rear bumper, were incorporated in the GTE for ease of development. John Crosthwaite himself undertook the task of modifying the Coupé chassis to fit the new body design. This was his speciality, in view of his previous experience with Cooper, Lotus and BRM. An initial plan to merely increase the wheelbase of the Coupé chassis by 7in and provide location for wider axles proved feasible and the prototype GTE had such an extended ladder chassis, but there was no space for the rear passengers' feet with this arrangement. Peter Bailey still runs this car (NRF 845F) now powered by a Ford V8 engine found lurking in the factory from an earlier, abandoned, project (the SE3?).

GTE prototype on extended Coupé chassis, note Coupé 15in wheels.

Rear view of GTE prototype shows original air vents above rear window instead of adjacent to rear lights on production cars.

In order to allow more footwell space, John drew up a completely new frame, not unlike the one David Page had designed for the contemporary Anadol (FW5). Both chassis possessed more than a passing resemblance to that of the Triumph Herald, in that the central cruciform theme was formed by deflecting the main 6in × 4in chassis box sections inwards to join at the centre of the car. At either end of the frame these main rails maintained a parallel configuration, braced with tubular and channel section cross-members. Lighter 3in × 2in channel section outriggers, connected by outer sill rails, formed a perimeter structure to support the bodywork and provide some measure of protection, not present in earlier designs, from side-swipe type collisions. The rearmost outriggers were of heavy tubular construction since the front seat-belt anchorages were sited at the outer ends, which were adjacent to the front pivots for the rear axle trailing arms. These arms were now 8in longer than on the Coupé, allowing 7.7in of wheel movement as opposed to the 5.75in of the earlier car, without inducing any undesirable steering effects on uneven surfaces. The new GTE was only 3in longer overall than the Coupé at 171in, but its wheelbase was 8in greater. Similarly, the larger car was 2in wider, but the front and rear tracks were 4in and 3in wider respectively. This re-arrangement of the chassis components gave the GTE a far more stable stance, with the effect of a wheel at each corner and minimal overhang.

Substantial box-section chassis featured a well located rear axle and coil spring/damper units all round.

GRAND TOURING ESTATE

Robust Triumph-based front suspension.

The TR6 based front suspension was retained, but by mounting the double wishbone units further apart it was necessary to use a longer and sturdier steering rack. Some research round the British Leyland parts bins revealed that the Austin 1800 unit came nearest to the required specification of length and gearing. However, in the BL application the rack was placed behind the wheel centres, whereas Reliant had to locate it ahead of the front hubs. The simple answer was to employ a left-hand drive rack and turn it upside down to achieve the correct direction of operation. Spring rates were raised from 140lb/in to 160lb/in, because of the increase in body weight of 120lb and the larger carrying capacity. This naturally resulted in firmer suspension, compensated for by more stable cornering ability. In line with the current trend in the late 1960s, wheel sizes were reduced from 15in to 14in diameter, while their width increased from 5in to 5½in. This contrasts with the present fashion of larger diameter wheels and lower profile tyres.

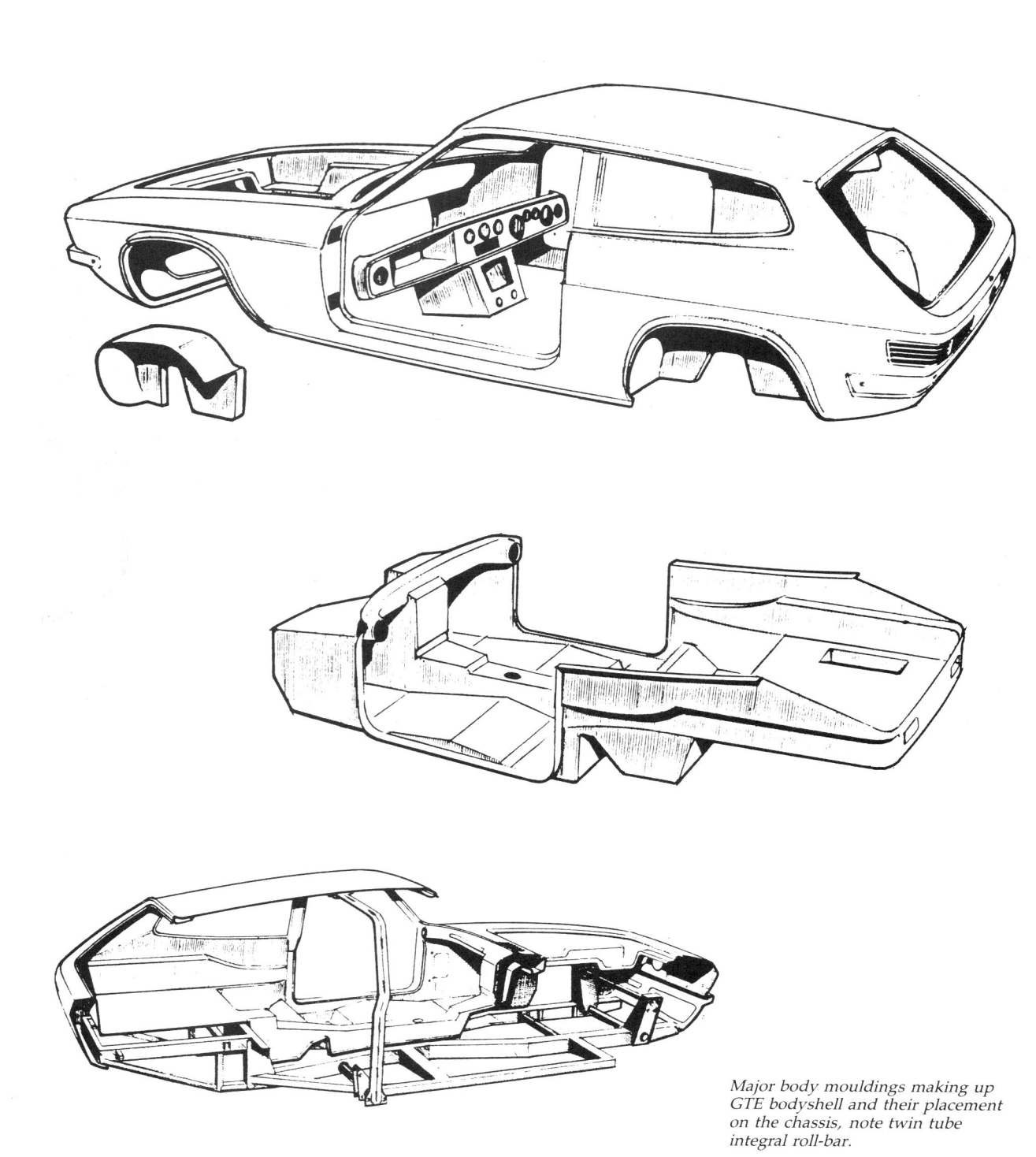

Major body mouldings making up GTE bodyshell and their placement on the chassis, note twin tube integral roll-bar.

Cutaway GTE at the 1968 Motor Show.

Increasing the wheelbase of a given layout can have an unfavourable effect on the weight distribution on the individual axles. In the case of the GTE, re-positioning the V6 engine further back in the chassis than in the Coupé only partially compensated for the 8in greater gap between the front and rear wheels. The situation was further aggravated by Reliant's decision to emulate Ford in their Zephyr/Zodiac Mk IV design by placing the spare wheel ahead of the compact V6 engine and above the new cross-flow radiator buried below. That engine and its associated gearbox was also derived from the same Ford models, but the Scimitar gained far more from this clever packaging under the bonnet as no extra front overhang was necessary and the rear section of the cabin was freed for passengers or luggage. The 17 gallon fuel tank was neatly stowed at the rear of the chassis below the load area, where the earlier Scimitar had housed its spare wheel.

The advanced external shape of the GTE concealed an equally pioneering internal layout, inspired by Ray Wiggin, who suggested that the individual rear seats should be made to fold separately. Such versatility enabled progressively more luggage to be carried, depending on whether both or only one of the rear seats were occupied. While the hatchback concept of an opening rear window or door to gain access to the passenger compartment had been seen earlier in the Austin A40 Countryman and Renault 16, the GTE broke new ground with its rear seating arrangement. Such a layout is now commonplace in all hatchbacks of any size or price or country of origin. Some of the design features of the GTE, not surprisingly, did not meet with universal approval, but 20 years later virtually every manufacturer in the world embodies one or more of these ideas in their own products. Apart from the split rear seating, now also used in some saloons, the rising waistline is almost universal in modern car profiles, while the rear lip of the Scimitar's roofline has been adapted into a distinctive spoiler on the sporting variants of every mass-produced car.

First version of GTE with 'spoked' fibreglass wheel trims.

GRAND TOURING ESTATE

Luggage capacity with different rear seat configurations.

Reclining front seats of similar design to those in the Sunbeam Alpine were supplied by Restall and trimmed in Reliant's own trim shop in black vinyl to match the all black interior decor as featured in the Coupé. The excellent facia layout of the earlier car was also retained, with the addition of eye-ball vents at either end to provide a measure of through-flow ventilation, following Ford's successful system in the Cortina. Corresponding air outlets were placed at the extreme rear corners of the car in line with the rear light clusters, which keen observers will, no doubt, realise were borrowed from the Hillman Hunter range. However, the GTE was in excellent company with this choice, as Aston Martin used the same units at the rear of their very up-market DBS model. Front twin headlamps incorporating side lamps followed the 1960s trend and were the same Lucas parts found on the Vauxhall Victor, whose indicator lights were also used.

Reliant's ability to rapidly modify production specification when necessary was demonstrated by the means of supporting the chrome-framed opening rear window. Initially a complicated arrangement of levers and springs, concealed behind the rear trim panels, performed this task for the first 17 cars off the line. A much neater, and cheaper, means was then adopted, employing two gas-filled springs rather like very slim shock absorbers which have since become essential equipment in all rear door or boot applications.

Spring-loaded struts were used initially to support rear window.

Motive power for the GTE was identical with that used in the last of the Coupés and only the cooling system of the sturdy 3-litre Zodiac V6 engine had to be altered by virtue of the low level cross-flow radiator, necessitating a remote header tank placed on the offside of the engine bay alongside the washer reservoir. These components took the place of one of the two 6-volt batteries used in the Coupé, now replaced by one 12-volt pack on the nearside. The engine compartment of the GTE was now far more crowded than its predecessor and accessibility suffered accordingly, particularly as the engine was sited even further back into the bulkhead and was covered with an assortment of metal shields in the hope of attaining some degree of radio suppression.

It is quite amazing that such a radical re-design by a small team within 12 months should then prove effective, reasonably reliable and eventually very popular. As Churchill might have put it "rarely has so much been produced so well, by so few, so quickly."

The pressure of work among all departments had been considerable and as a test and in order to recover from these pressures, John Crosthwaite and his wife took a pre-production GTE (PRE 162G) overland to Athens via the Brindisi-Patra ferry in September 1968. The car never missed a beat and turned heads all along the route. They slept in it, camped from it and stayed in the best hotels with it, yet the GTE never looked out of place. Despite the long distances and average speeds in the 60s, the couple never felt tired or stiff and arrived back just before the Motor Show with only one problem — a constantly dirty back window.

Rear seats could be individually folded to optimise space utilisation.

GRAND TOURING ESTATE

The introduction of the GTE (termed the SE5) at the 1968 Motor Show in London aroused considerable interest and for once it could be honestly said that it was the Reliant stand which must have given inspiration for numerous later designs rather than the reverse. In this writer's view, the decision by Ray Wiggin to pursue this design was almost as brave and influential as that of Leonard Lord when he gave the go-ahead to produce Alec Issigonis's revolutionary Mini. Even though the latter was far more fundamental in overall car design, the relative importance of each model to both companies, in view of their vast difference in size, was comparable.

Cutaway GTE at its launch.

Superimposed outline of GTE over the Coupé

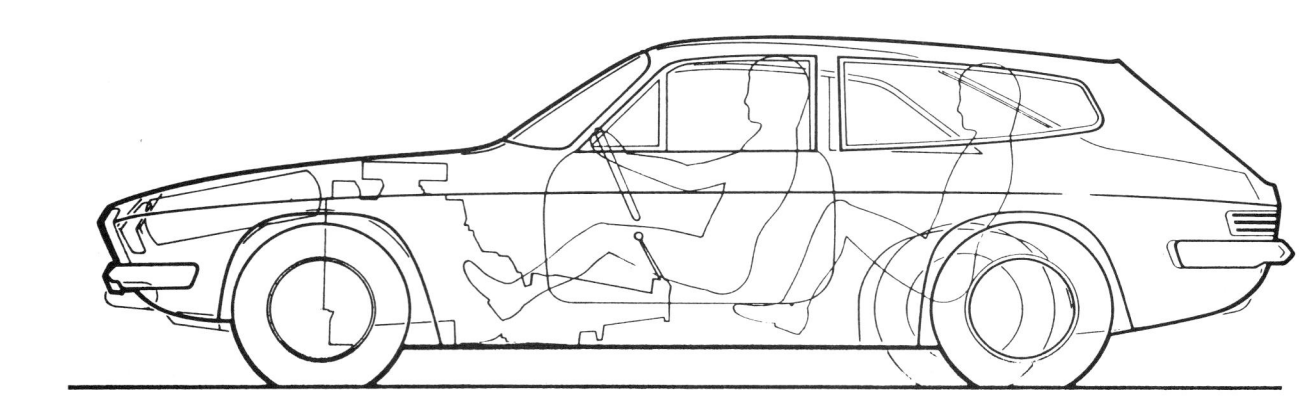

The GTE was immediately a distinctive car in both appearance and ability, with its cleverly sculptured rear quarters producing a very sporting flavour to a basically estate car format. The car caught the eye of any observer and quite definitely stood out from the herd. The shape was not always favourably received and tended to split the motoring fraternity into those who loved it and the others who loathed it. Whereas the Coupé was widely accepted as an elegant, if rather bland looking, machine, its successor had far more dramatic and forceful lines. Behind the wheel the similiarities of the basic design were apparent, although the GTE, with improved visibility, naturally felt far more spacious. The performance of the new car was marginally down and the handling not quite so spritely, due to the increase in total weight and its distribution at the wheels. The 50:50 laden weight distribution of the Coupé produced a very balanced car, but the longer wheelbase and wider track of the GTE gave it far more ultimate stability during cornering as well as during high speed cruising, even in the cross winds. This was a further tribute to Ogle's design, which had never seen a wind tunnel.

Ogle in the meantime were determined to capitalise on the impact of their new design inspiration by exhibiting their own version of the new Scimitar on their stand at the same show. Calling it the Ogle GTE, Tom Karen and his team incorporated additional features such as retractable headlamp covers and glazed roof section over the front seats, which gave an even smoother shape to the car. A nice finishing touch, now seen in the Porsche 928 for instance, was to mould the name OGLE into the fibreglass bodywork on either side, in place of separate badges clipped into place. This excellent use of the plastic material is an elegant application of the medium, yet very cheap to incorporate and resistant to removal by accident or vandals. This unique car was used for a time by Mrs. Julian Hodge, wife of the Chairman of the Hodge Group which owned Reliant.

GRAND TOURING ESTATE

Revolutionary profile of the GTE.

Ogle's special version of the GTE, also shown at the 1968 Motor Show, incorporated retractable headlamp covers.

When it comes to drawing comparisons of performance with contemporary models one has difficulty in finding a direct competitor offering so much versatility. Reliant had been so successful in finding a gap in the market for performance cars that it could not be directly assessed against outright two seater sports cars on one hand or large estate cars on the other. 'Motor' magazine chose the following three cars for comparison purposes in their 1969 road test summaries:

	Scimitar GTE	Alfa 1750 GTV	BMW 2000Ti	Daimler SP250
Capacity (cc)	2,994	1,798	1,990	2,500
Max speed (mph)	113.2	110	113.5	108
0-50mph (secs)	7.7	7.0	7.2	8.1
mpg (overall)	19.2	23.4	22.0	18.0
Price (£)	1,823	1,898	1,999	1,739

Richard Baker announcing the GTE bodyshell at the 'Most Beautiful Body of 1970' contest.

On its first anniversary, at the 1969 Motor Show, the GTE still had no pretender to share its unique sector of the market, but Reliant were not resting on their laurels and were responding to comments made by the press and public during its brief career. Two modifications appeared at its second showing, both concentrated at the rear of the car. Firstly, to cure the rapidity with which the rear window became opaque with dirt on wet roads a bottom-pivoting wiper was neatly inserted in the panel below this tailgate screen and a washer was added at the same time to assist the wiper in its cleaning action. These features were another first from Reliant, since copied by every manufacturer offering fastback or estate models. The vertical fuel filler, also in the same panel, was the subject of some criticism as its connection to the fuel tank by a right-angled hose restricted the speed of filling to an annoying extent. In a typical response to such problems, Reliant simply replaced the former Humber Sceptre filler cap with a side-hinged component fitted at such an angle that the path into the fuel tank was now straight, providing unrestricted and rapid filling. This property was very important with such a large tank, allowing over 400 miles of non-stop motoring.

A rear screen wiper and washer were soon introduced and the fuel filler was modified to facilitate filling.

In addition to these corrective changes in the specification, an automatic transmission option was offered for the first time in any Reliant product, in the form of the trusty Borg-Warner 35 box employed by Ford and many other British manufacturers. The combination of these changes and a rapidly established reputation no doubt contributed to orders of over £1 million being taken at the 1969 exhibition at Earls Court.

The Coupé was still retained on the price list and production continued until 1970, very much in the shadow of its bigger brother. Clearly its popularity was bound to decline due to its restricted carrying capacity and dated appearance. The real cause of the Coupé's demise was sheer lack of production capacity now required to keep up with the increasing demand for the SE5, which precluded the continued use of manpower and space for the smaller car.

Tom Scott (left) celebrates with Ray Wiggin the flood of orders at the 1969 Motor Show.

GRAND TOURING ESTATE

An undoubted boost to the status and reputation of the GTE occurred in 1970 when the press were humming with reports of HRH The Princess Anne being seen driving a new, Satin Silver Scimitar around London. The car had been loaned by the Kenning Group for Princess Anne to try, probably after her father's favourable experiences with the Ogle GTS, which of course had similar origins. The outcome of this trial proved of immense importance to Reliant, who shortly afterwards received an order for a GTE from Buckingham Palace. This was to be a joint birthday and Christmas present for Princess Anne from her parents and other members of the Royal family. Her 'Aircraft Blue' SE5, trimmed in light grey leather, was to be the first of a succession of Scimitars to be owned by Princess Anne, all carrying her cherished registration 1420 H, referring to her position as Colonel-in-Chief of the Royal 14/20th Hussars.

HRH The Princess Anne with her own Scimitar outside the Reliant offices.

Reliant were not complacent over the successful introduction of the SE5 and gave the model a facelift for the October 1971 Motor Show and in line with earlier labelling the revised car was termed the SE5a. Externally, the headlights were raised 2in to comply with new vehicle regulations at home and abroad, while the dummy grille between them was now a one-piece casting comprising seven bars in place of the four separate strips of the SE5. The bright waistline strips were replaced by a painted coachline, complemented by a polished strip along the bottom of each sill. Additional bright mouldings at the top of the door panel completed the line already produced by the rear side windows. The final change in the detailed cosmetics involved replacing the shield badge on the front with a larger version and also applying this badge to the flanks behind the front wheels in place of the original '3 litre' badges. The body letters underwent a change to a shorter, but fatter, type-style. From the rear the SE5a was easily identified by the tidier light arrangement in which the two light clusters now incorporated the reversing lamps, and the new assemblies were again shared by Aston Martin on their new DBS V8 models, as well as by the TVR M series and the Jensen Healey.

New rear light unit incorporating reversing lights were introduced in 1972.

The SE5a was introduced in 1972 featuring a new grille and Dunlop composite alloy wheels.

The earlier cast alloy wheels available as an optional extra gave way to a composite wheel made by Dunlop consisting of an alloy centre rivetted to a chrome plated steel rim. While very attractive when clean and polished these were difficult to keep in that condition and were sometimes difficult to balance. A revised fibreglass wheel trim was fitted to the standard steel wheels which were now easily mistaken for alloy wheels as well as being very practical. Less noticeable was the change of door handle from Ford Cortina origin to a British Leyland source in common with the rear hatch lock.

More dramatic changes took place inside the passenger compartment in which all the fixed trim panels were now vacuum-formed mouldings made from ABS plastic instead of padded vinyl-covered surfaces. The facia moulding was far more modern-looking even if it was less ergonomic than its predecessor when it came to the control layout. As well as giving a more professional appearance to the interior it was no doubt cheaper to make since production figures had grown sufficiently for moulded panels to be a viable proposition. An alternative to the universal black decor was now available in the form of tan upholstery and fittings, further enhanced by the choice of leather facings to the seats as an option. Safety rocker type switches replaced the toggle variety, but placing them in a line caused much confusion during night driving, with the adjacent and identical light and wiper controls being particularly disconcerting. The earlier central heater in the engine compartment was abandoned in favour of a unit borrowed from the Triumph 1300 range inside the car, while the blower motors were placed in each footwell and the fresh air outlets appeared, less sensibly, in the centre of the facia. These changes certainly improved the showroom appeal of the Scimitar, but have proved less durable over long periods of use and exposure to the sun's rays, which seem to affect the brown interiors more than the black. The materials used and their method of manufacture have also rendered restoration more difficult than the plainer, hand made SE5 interiors.

The revised moulded facia of the SE5a.

Few mechanical changes accompanied these cosmetic improvements incorporated in the SE5a. The roll centre of the front suspension was lowered slightly by moving down the inner pivot points of the bottom wishbones, while the rear axle was now the stronger 4HA variety. These axles, supplied by Salisbury transmissions, were unique to the Scimitar even though the differential assembly was common to several other axles of the same origin fitted to other high performance cars such as Jaguar, Aston Martin and the Sunbeam Tiger. The rear axle on the GTE has often proved to be the Achilles heel of the older cars, not because of any lack of strength or design fault, but largely due to lack of diligent maintenance at some stage of the car's life. They have a history of leaking front oil seals, peculiar to the Scimitar application, rendering it imperative to maintain adequate oil level. Failure to observe this precaution has led to the demise of so many of these robust, and expensive, components. Equally, the lack of correct lubrication of the lower front suspension trunnions has caused many a Scimitar to become an involuntary three-wheeler, with consequent costly damage.

Only a year after the SE5 received its first revision to the SE5a, Reliant had to adopt the later, up-rated 3-litre V6 engine following Ford's introduction of this revised unit in the 1972 Granada range. Internally the new engine received a stiffer block casting and improved 'D' shaped ports for the cylinder heads and manifold, allowing better gas flow assisted by a higher-lift camshaft. These changes produced a freer revving engine capable of developing about 5bhp more. Inspection of the specification of the GTE with the corresponding Ford model will reveal a lower power output figure by about 4bhp, which is entirely attributable to the restrictive cast iron exhaust manifolds fitted by Reliant to avoid the footwells, which are very close to the rear cylinders of each bank of the V6 unit. The external changes made to the Granada engine presented the Reliant Engineering Department with a few problems, however. Firstly, the well in the sump was now to the rear of the engine, necessitating the substitution of a strategic tubular chassis cross-member with a plate beneath the new sump, bolted to the underside of each chassis rail. New engine mountings were accommodated by revised brackets welded on top of, rather than on, the inner faces of the main chassis members. The earlier Zodiac had its cooling fan mounted on the front end of the crankshaft, so that it aligned with the low-mounted radiator below the spare wheel. In the Granada the spare wheel was conventionally in the boot, so the radiator and its fan now rose from the depths to a higher location. Changes to the front cover of the engine meant the dipstick, previously in the front, now sprouted from the offside of the block — far less accessible in the GTE. Furthermore, the cooling fan could not be placed high up as in the Granada, so a thermostatically controlled Wood-Jefferies electric fan was mounted ahead of the radiator, and the cross tube between the front suspension turrets was re-shaped to avoid the redundant fan pulley. This did offer the benefit of a quieter engine, free from the need to drive a cooling fan at all times, but an option was offered to fit the early crank-driven fan for towing applications.

Allied to the engine revision was a gearbox change. Ford abandoned the 2604E overdrive box in its large cars, leaving Reliant in somewhat of a quandary as it deprived the GTE of its characteristic long-legged gait. Their immediate reaction was to utilise the new 2614E 'Bullit' box and cable clutch from the Granada and raise the rear axle ratio from 3.31:1 to the Jaguar E-type ratio of 3.07:1, as used on the early automatic cars too. The resultant top gear was little different from the previous overdrive top while the higher second gear of the Granada box was a distinct advantage. However, the bottom gear was now quite high, which gave some problems when hill-starting while towing in the GTE. Reliant were not content with this situation and adopted a hybrid overdrive gearbox, similar to that offered by Ford in their Special Vehicle Option 3-litre Transits used by the police and ambulance brigades. However, the Granada gear cluster conveniently fitted into this gearbox casing and the step-up ratio of the Laycock J-type overdrive was adjusted to suit the GTE. For some reason Reliant decided, contrary to Ford practice, to retain a hydraulic clutch with a combination of Girling and Lockheed components. The debit side of this combination revealed itself in the remote gearchange borrowed from the pre-1972 Capri 3-litre, which left much to be desired in its mode of action and feel, in contrast to the delightful, positive gearchange of the manual, no-overdrive GTE's using the standard Granada gearbox. Thus for the rest of the production life of the SE5a, until 1975, three transmission options were available, giving the following performance figures as issued by the makers:

SE5a	Manual 4-speed	Manual O/drive	Automatic
Max speed (mph)	123	123	120
0-60mph (secs)	8.6	8.9	9.8
Standing-¼ mile (sec)	16.4	16.8	17.6
mpg (at 70mph)	30	30.5	27
Price (£)	2,348	2,398	2,487

Having driven all these variations, the author is in no doubt that the manual four-speed cars are the most pleasant of all to drive, as well as offering marginally better performance and the prospect of a more trouble-free life.

The SE5 was always a reasonably well-equipped motor car, with options limited to radio, heated rear window and laminated windscreen. The introduction of the SE5a saw several more options appear

Grand Touring Estate

Two very attractive models.

on the price list, including chrome-rimmed alloy wheels, stereo 8-track player, leather upholstery, electric windows, tinted glass and fog and spot lamps. Many cars were fitted with folding sun roofs, of which only the Webasto make were approved by Reliant, and even that version involved cutting through the twin steel tube roll-over bar moulded into the roof panel, but a timber frame around the opening retained much of the original strength.

Artist's impression of the new Two Gates factory required for Scimitar and three-wheeler production.

Demand for the GTE meant that production had to be carried out on similar lines to that of the three-wheelers. The bodies were moulded at the Kettlebrook glassfibre works near Tamworth town centre. Chassis, welded-up at Two Gates, were transported to Kettlebrook and mated with the bodies, both components being suspended on their side for this operation. The combined unit now passed through the paint bay before being ferried back to Two Gates for final assembly. Here the bodies were lifted off their chassis and given a further coat of paint, while the running gear was fitted to the also re-painted bare chassis travelling along a small production line. Finally, the bodies were reunited with their respective fully-equipped chassis for trimming, inspection and testing.

The arrival of the SE5a saw production rise from 28 to 50 per week during 1972, and further small improvements were added to the GTE specification for the 1973 Motor Show. These included a folding tonneau to cover the luggage area (since copied by makers of modern hatchbacks) and the fitting of rear seat belts as standard, ten years before such items appeared on comparable cars. No doubt helped by the efforts of Sales Director Tom Scott, the number of Scimitars sold in 1973 rose to around 2,000. On this successful note Tom retired, after 20 years in the same crucial post within the company, which he had joined 27 years previously as an engineer following demobilisation from the RAF.

The success of the GTE had not gone unnoticed by some other manufacturers, notably Volvo, who launched a pretender to the Scimitar in their 1800ES model in 1972. This was virtually an estate version of their P1800 Coupé, made famous by the TV 'Saint' series, and its evolution can be compared with that of the Scimitar Coupé. However, it was not a thorough re-design as in the case of the GTE, so even though luggage capacity was increased and access to it was via an opening, rear, frameless glass window, seating capacity was still only enough for two adults and two very small children. The Volvo, although better looking in some eyes, was not a success and was withdrawn after only a few years in production, presumably because it could not compete with the GTE in convenience, performance or indeed charisma. Ironically, some 12 years later, the Swedish company have re-entered the same sector of the market with their 480ES front-wheel drive range of sporting estate cars, now that the Scimitar is no longer made.

Despite the new competition, sales of the GTE continued to rise to around 2,500 per annum for 1974 and 1975. The highest monthly sales of 248 were recorded in August 1975, which was a 9.7% improvement over the same month in 1974 when 226 were sold. This represented a 14.3% increase in its share of the specialist UK car market. In order to satisfy these record level of sales, production methods had to be streamlined, particularly in the time-consuming moulding process.

Thus during the latter period of its production life the bodyshells were cured in heated tunnels alongside the three-wheeler models. This more rapid curing process did little for the quality of the finished mouldings, and a certain amount of rippling sometimes occurred along the sides of the bodies, which detracted somewhat from the excellent fit of the panels themselves.

1975 was the last full year in which the SE5a was manufactured, but it was a memorable one for the workforce, who were honoured with a visit by HRH The Princess Anne on 15th July when she arrived in her third GTE which was only a few weeks old, at the Two Gates factory. One of her more amusing quotes was in answer to Toolroom Foreman Tommy Chetwynd's comment that he had been at Reliant for 38 years when she responded by asking "do you think you will stay?". A month later, Mrs. Thatcher, then Leader of the Opposition,

HRH The Princess Anne visiting the Reliant production line in 1975.

also toured the Reliant factories at Two Gates, Shenstone and Kettlebrook. Diplomatic as ever, she declared that she would love to own a GTE if only she had the money — hardly a quip she could use today, one presumes. The prestige conferred on the Scimitar by its royal patronage was further substantiated by its attraction to numerous show business personalities not known for being short of funds such as David Nixon (HPG 2K) and Noel Edmonds (MOY 292L). These days, no doubt, their cars would carry cherished registration numbers and like most manufacturers Reliant captured suitable identities for their works demonstration cars, of which the following are examples: 1GTE, RMC 1L, RMC 5L, RMC 6L, RMC 7L and RMC 9L (RMC standing for Reliant Motor Company, of course).

In those buoyant mid 1970s, the Scimitar seemed to thrive on the growing competition from sporting four seaters. It was able to hold its own in performance as well as offering versatility, durability and distinctive styling, which the following figures cannot portray:

	SE5a	Triumph Stag	Capri 3000	Volvo P1800ES	Elan +2
Capacity (cc)	2,994	2,997	2,994	1,985	1,558
Max speed (mph)	121	121	122	110.5	121
0-60mph (sec)	8.9	9.7	8.3	9.7	7.5
mpg (typical)	24	25	22	25	28
Weight (cwt)	21.8	25.9	22.5	23.1	17.2
Price (£)	2,397	2,177	1,824	2,651	2,659

Noel Edmonds with his new acquisition.

Reliant's enthusiastic Managing Director was not one to rest on his laurels and he listened to the various criticisms made of the SE5a with characteristic care. The main adverse comments concerned the lack of room for four large adults and their luggage, and the firmness of the suspension. The Scimitar offered more internal space than the Capri, even if its ride was harder and the handling benefited from such suspension settings. The GTE had set out initially to be a sports car primarily, but having the benefit of carrying capacity previously unheard of in a sporting car. The very success of the model, and its status, had attracted buyers from the executive market who had sporting aspirations and enjoyed the distinctive qualities of the big Reliant, but nevertheless hankered for the luxury normally associated with senior management cars. Ray Wiggin and his co-directors felt that this was the market they should be pursuing and discussions took place with Tom Karen on ways to enlarge the GTE without altering its basic appearance and character. That trend of thought resulted in the SE5a becoming the last real sporting model to come out of the Two Gates factory for at least eight years and remains, in the author's mind, as the definitive Scimitar.

Mrs. Thatcher, then Leader of the Opposition, visiting the Reliant factory.

GRAND TOURING ESTATE

The appeal of the GTE was not confined to these shores, as several examples were exported to the Benelux countries, Scandinavia, Switzerland (36 cars), Australia, New Zealand and South Africa. Several Scimitars have been privately imported into the USA, where spares availability must present some problems.

There is no denying that the car was becoming long in the tooth in various aspects of its design, primarily as far as the interior and the controls were concerned. The fairly basic reclining front seats were in need of replacement by more modern, anatomically acceptable, equipment, while the minor controls were never very ergonomic in layout. Externally, the overall body shape was still as appealing as ever, proving almost timeless in profile. Detailed areas such as the separate chrome bumpers and fussy door windows could certainly have benefited from some re-design without detracting from the balanced compact nature of the car. Some tuning applied to the engine, particularly the exhaust system, and an improved gear change for the overdrive models would certainly have enhanced the driving pleasure of the GTE, even though an increasing number of buyers were now opting for automatic transmission, indicating its growing up-market appeal. The front suspension, although quite

The GTE has always been a favourite with 'high fliers'.

effective when carefully maintained, was derived from a 1948 design for the Triumph Mayflower and was not capable of endowing the much heavier GTE with the versatility offered by more modern arrangements. There were good arguments indeed for expanding the Scimitar range into an executive 'L' model and a more sporting 'S' variant, along the lines followed by its mass-produced brethren. In this way luxurious fitments such as air-conditioning, extra sound deadening and superior trimming would appease the business buyer, while more engine power, wider wheels and tyres allied to superior suspension damping would continue to attract the sports car enthusiast.

Reliant decided, however, that an entirely new bodyshell was required to achieve continued market penetration without any alteration to the running gear — very much a case of 'old wine in a new bottle'. Admittedly, by most standards, the wine was good vintage for its day, but it did not improve with keeping.

This 6.7-litre, supercharged Chrysler engined GTE custom car won the 'Best Competition Car' at two custom shows in 1973.

The Scimitar matures

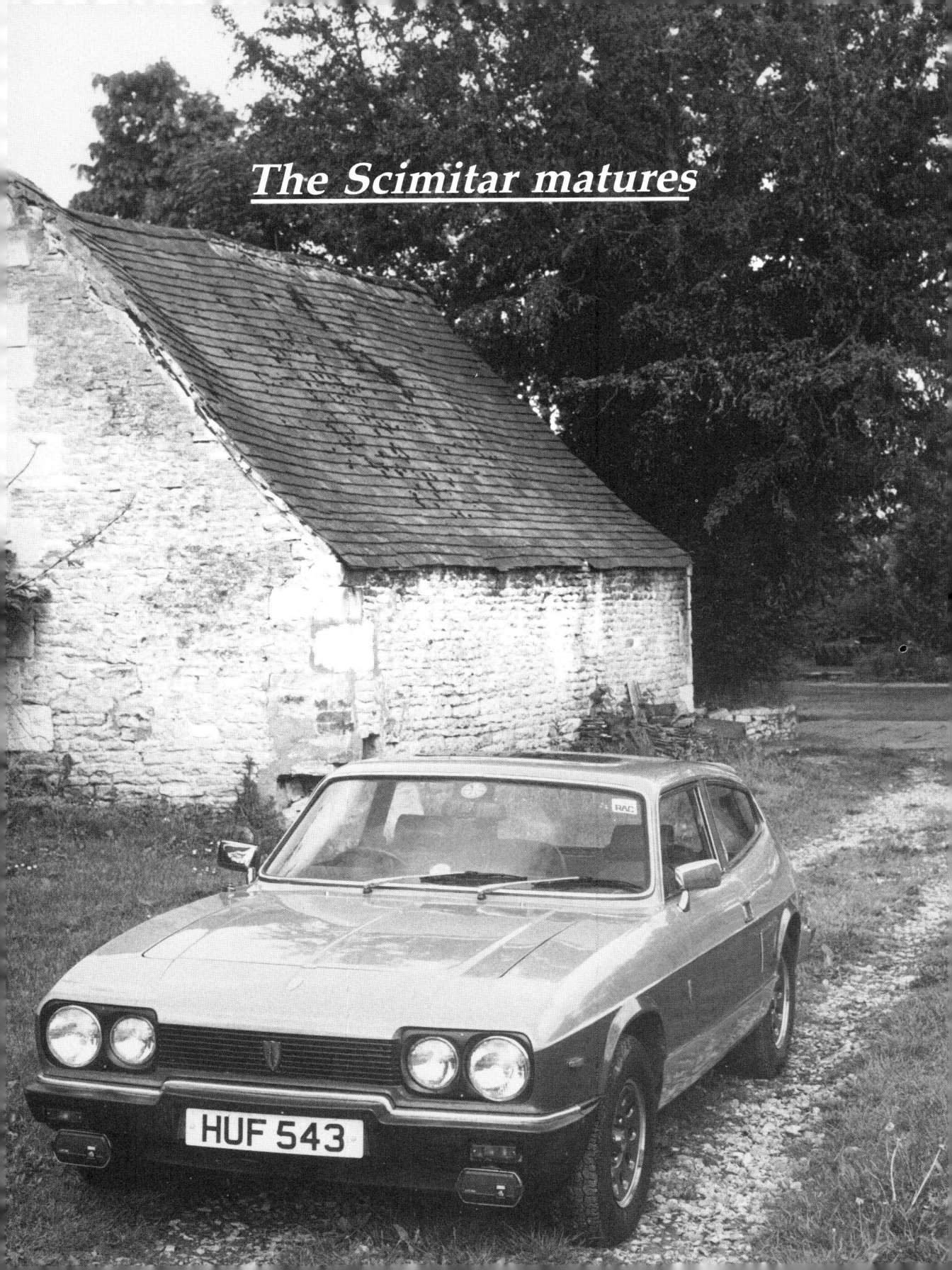

Which Director has more drive?

If you're of the opinion that the car you drive reflects the kind of person you are, reflect on this.

Scimitar GTE is the epitome of style in a high performance estate. It can carry 4 adults and at least 20 cubic feet of luggage (40 cubic feet with both rear seats folded forward) at up to 120 mph. Quietly. Comfortably.

So the person in control needs to be able to handle power. Responsibly.

Scimitar regularly returns between 24 and 28 mpg (although many owners claim over 30 mpg). At that rate, its 20 gallon tank gives it a non-stop range of over 500 miles. Obviously, instead of wasting expensive energy, Scimitar owners use it. To their own advantage.

As well as being original in concept, Scimitar looks unique. It's long, low and wide. With rustproof handbuilt coachwork mounted on a rugged steel chassis.

As you see, a Scimitar GTE is practical as well as stylish. An individual car built by an independent British Company for individualists. A car of considerable resourcefulness.

Exactly like the person who owns it. If this advertisement has proved you to be such a person, we have a suggestion.

Steal a perfectly legitimate march on your colleagues and get more details now.

After all, you've proved you're a person with certain natural advantages. And when you have an advantage, why give it away.

To: Marketing Services, Reliant Motor Company Ltd, Tamworth, Staffs B77 1HN
or phone Tamworth (0827) 69595 any time.

☐ Please send me more details about the Scimitar GTE
☐ Please arrange a road test.   ☐ If under 18 tick here.

Name
Address

Present car

RELIANT SCIMITAR GTE
High performance estate

SM/1

The Reliant Scimitar GTE. 138 bhp 3 litre Ford V6 Engine. Manual overdrive or automatic transmission. Rack and pinion steering (power optional). Servo assisted front disc brakes. 2 speed wipers with electric washers front and rear. Heated, wide opening rear window. Complete instrumentation. Remote control exterior mirror. Radio (radio cassette optional). Low profile radial tyres (alloy wheels optional). Fabric upholstery (leather optional). Reclining front seats with seat belts front and rear. Dual exhaust system. Electric radiator fan. Through-flow ventilation with multiple outlet points. Laminated windscreen, tinted glass and electric windows optional.

CHAPTER 6

The Scimitar matures

RAY WIGGIN WAS anxious to respond to criticisms of the lack of space and comfort in the SE5a, so a development programme was set into action in late 1974. Experiments on the SE5a bodywork to achieve these aims were undertaken initially by Ken Wood, head of the Reliant Development Department. In order to assess the dimensions which were likely to satisfy future buyers, they cut in half an SE5 bodyshell in line with the rear of the door opening and inserted 4in in the wheelbase, of which 2½in was added to the door width and the remaining 1½in inserted between the door aperture and the wheel arches. While this extension provided sufficient leg room for adult rear passengers, shoulder room was still limited for large people. A further dissection process down the centre line of the car was now performed and the two halves of the shell were mounted on a platform so that they could be moved apart to ascertain the ideal interior width. Eventually an increase of 3in was found to fill the bill and a strip of fibreglass of that width inserted into the gap to unite the split bodyshell once again. Since front seat widths were unaltered, only the centre console was widened, thus offering the desired extra elbow room. The rear seat was now converted to a bench cushion over a flattened central hump over the transmission present in the SE5/5a, permitting three children to be accommodated. While the split backrests were retained, the central armrest no longer featured.

SE6 shape evolving from SE5 bodyshell in Development Department.

Having arrived at a new set of body dimensions by trial and error, Reliant naturally placed the task of revamping the overall design of the GTE in the hands of Ogle Design, who created the original shape. Tom Karen welcomed the increased width of the new specification, but was less happy about the extension of the wheelbase from the aesthetic point of view. Enlarging the door width without altering the size of the rear quarterlights upset the fine balance of the SE5 profile. Eliminating the front hinging quarterlights from the doors cleaned up the appearance slightly, but the extended length of the total glass area, of the same depth as before, tended to give the effect of a narrower proportion of glass to bodywork and thus a higher waistline. This in turn slightly reduced the effect of a rising lower window line as well as flattening the attractive sculpturing around the flanks above the rear wheel arches. In an attempt to break up the increased expanse of bodywork and reduce any slab-sided impresssion, a rib was inserted along the side panels and doors in line with the top of the new, black rubber covered, bumpers. The latter were certainly an improvement both aesthetically and functionally over the chromed steel components of the SE5. As well as affording greater protection for the fibreglass panels front and rear, small impacts would not leave their mark and their absence of corrosion matched that of the rest of the bodywork. Most of the remaining brightwork was now composed of polished aluminium or stainless steel, which also would not suffer from terminal rust.

Profile shows cleaner shape due to absence of front quarterlights and integral rubber bumpers.

The Scimitar Matures

The close fit of the new bumper assemblies helped to give the car a more professional appearance and accentuated the long, low stance of the car. However, the finalising of the frontal aspect gave Tom Karen and his team almost as many problems as the SE5 had done formerly. Experimental layouts using four 5¾in headlamps, as on the SE5, were tried initially, but they now looked too small, so four 7in units were inserted, before a compromise of two outer 7in and two inner 5¾in lamps finally found favour. To complement the black bumpers, the grille was now a black plastic moulding surmounted by a narrow bright stainless strip carrying the Scimitar name. This matched the thin stainless extrusions inserted around the top edge of the bumper to provide a boundary between it and the painted bodywork. The black theme was extended below bumper level where the air intake and optional driving lamps were incorporated in a front spoiler-type detachable moulding. A similarly removable moulding was fitted at the rear carrying an identical rubber bumper as well as high-intensity rear fog lamps and the number plate. The corner outlet body vents were now accentuated by black plastic coverings housing side reflectors, in line with the rear lamps, also with black surrounds emphasising the greater width of the new body.

Larger outer headlamps and rubber bumper distinguish SE6 from its predecessor.

The new car, logically to be known as the SE6, was a more imposing and smoother looking vehicle than the SE5a, but lacked the more rounded, sculptured appearance of its predecessor, now that the sides were flatter and the front profile less pointed. Ogle Design achieved far greater success with their treatment of the interior of the revised model. The facia moulding, now in black, was far more impressive and a little more ergonomic, even though similar instruments and controls were fitted, apart from two column stalks, one of which now controlled the front wipers and washers. This new feature and the circular display of warning lights were borrowed from the large Triumph cars. The central instrument display of five smaller gauges now occupied a separate panel from that housing the larger speedometer and tachometer directly in front of the driver. The face level vents had reverted to a more sensible position at the extreme ends of the dashboard, as on the earlier SE4 and SE5 models. All the hard trim, including the facia and door panels, was manufactured from vacuum formed ABS, as used on the SE5a, but was now available in tan or blue, contrasting tastefully with the black facia and steering wheel.

This SE6 facia has been specially trimmed in hand-stitched leather.

The Scimitar Matures

While the reclining seats were no wider than before, they were vastly more substantial and comfortable and slid as well as tipped forwards on releasing a catch on the outside edge of each backrest. This made access to the rear seats much easier, especially as the doors were now wider. The seats were upholstered as standard with nylon velour facings and vinyl surrounds in tan or blue and leather was an option as before. The rear seat backrests were still individually folding, even though the cushion was one piece without the dividing armrest so much appreciated in the rear of the SE5 series. The greater width of the SE6 yielded proportionally more luggage space, which amounted to 21cu ft, 30cu ft, or 40cu ft according to whether both, one or neither rear seats were occupied.

Hidden from the eye was an extra layer of sound-deadening rubber sponge glued to the interior surfaces of the whole body up to window level. This reduced engine and road noise considerably, allowing passengers to appreciate the performance of the new stereo cassette player to a greater degree than that of the obsolete eight-track players fitted to the earlier cars. Additional options, which brought the SE6 specification very much into line with its competitors, included headrests, electric windows and aerial, rear seat belts, internally adjustable door mirrors and a delay on the internal courtesy light switch.

Improved seating with nylon cloth facings featured in the SE6.

Not one single fibreglass or window panel of the SE6 was shared with the SE5, which must have brought development costs up to those of introducing an entirely new car, even though the overall appearance was very similar. The same plan of expanding the dimensions of an earlier car when designing its replacement was apparent among its closest sporting competitors, namely the Ford Capri and Datsun Z series. In each instance the revamped model employed completely new body panels to provide a more spacious interior, while losing the essential elegance and litheness of the original car. In so doing each car lost some of its sporting character while pandering to the tastes of the more mature prospective owner and moving the model up-market and away from the sector for which it was originally destined.

Quite clearly the new GTE was going to require a completely new chassis and this followed the SE5 unit closely in concept by siting the extended box-section main members 3in further apart, commensurate with the wider body. Identical suspension units were used at the front while the rear axle was merely a wider version of the SE5a Salisbury built 4HA variety, with the same 3.31:1 ratio differential. This was linked to the unchanged 3-litre V6 engine and gearbox by a longer propshaft, which was a split unit incorporating constant velocity joints in the case of the manual overdrive cars. A wider steering rack was necessary and the greater under bonnet space permitted the option of power assistance as well. The manual and power racks were derived from the BL Princess and Rover SD1 models respectively, having special tie rods to match the wishbone suspension geometry of the Scimitar. The spring rates of the suspension were altered to achieve a softer ride, while the SE5 Girling brakes were retained, actuated by a twin circuit system with integral servo assistance so that the front and rear brakes were on separate circuits. The wider chassis did permit Reliant to fit a 20 gallon fuel tank under the rear luggage space, some three gallons larger than on the SE5/5a models, but still one gallon less than the SE4/4a tank.

The heating system was up-rated by fitting a blower motor behind each pair of headlamps and this fed air through a constantly heated matrix behind the facia, with two interior controls to regulate temperature and direction of air flow. Reliant modified the cooling system to a sealed variety with an overflow bottle to accommodate any expansion of water which should then be sucked back into the engine on cooling. The pattern chosen sealed off any water circulation to the back of the inlet manifold from the water pump, as on all other applications of the Ford V6 engine including the earlier Scimitars, which seems to have endowed the SE6 with reputation for overheating, particularly on the older models.

The SE6 was introduced to the public at the 1975 Motor Show, when the SE5 was at the peak of its sales achievements. Its success

THE SCIMITAR MATURES

SE6 production line showing bodies being re-united with chassis.

looked set to be carried on by the new Scimitar as £3 million worth of orders were taken at its first showing, indicating the excellent showroom appeal of the new design. The number of new dealer applications also increased after the show, particularly from purveyors of prestige cars such as Lotus, Mercedes and Porsche, delighting the Reliant Board whose intention it had been to break into the executive market. The emphasis of the Scimitar had certainly changed, but so had the critical nature of the clientele who demanded standards of finish and reliability difficult to achieve with the resources of the Tamworth company. Reliant did not have the ability or equipment to test every aspect of the design to destruction and relied on their skill at assembling a wide range of mass-production componentry, which had already been proved in service. To a large extent, specialist car makers, such as Reliant, have to depend on an enthusiastic buyer who admires the product to the extent that he or she will tolerate minor troubles, particularly on models fresh from the drawing board and be prepared to wait for the manufacturer to sort out problems when they occur. To put it crudely, early customers of such cars tend to be an extension of the Development Department and must appreciate the limited amount of capital that can be afforded on this aspect, in view of the low volume of production and the overall value for money provided by such individual motor cars.

One area of the new design which gave immediate problems was the front suspension. In order to try and achieve a 'boulevard' ride, the settings chosen for the front springs and dampers were clearly too soft, as complaints of 'bottoming' and wallowy handling were voiced by new owners. Luckily Reliant were able to respond, with Girling's help, by offering uprated spring/damper units which could be easily replaced by undoing two bolts on each unit once the car was jacked up. Many such assemblies were changed under warranty, but already the problems of lack of development were becoming apparent. In addition to less precise handling, compared with the SE5a, the power steering system on the SE6 seemed to offer little feel of the road and was almost too light for the size of the car. The greater width and length of the basic chassis could not be expected to contribute to increased rigidity and resulted in a generally less taut feel from the driving seat. Creaks and groans were reported by early tests as evidence of the more flexible body and chassis movements. The larger, hence heavier, doors presented problems of premature dropping traced to lack of rigidity in the hinge support area of the door pillars, for which there was no easy remedy.

Fortunately the unchanged engine coupled to the overdrive gearbox still offered lusty performance with even more relaxed high-speed cruising than any previous Scimitar. The combination of better seating and additional sound-proofing was certainly appreciated by all who drove the SE6, even if there was an overall weight penalty of 140lb. The quality of the early Capri-type gear-change, as used in the late SE5a, was still a very unsatisfactory mechanism. In contrast, the adoption of the Ford C3 automatic in place of the venerable Borg Warner 35 box produced far smoother gear-changes, even if the reliability of the British made unit did not match the earlier American designed one.

The build up of teething troubles kept the Development Department fully occupied for many months and a number of revisions were incorporated into the SE6 after production had reached 1,550 cars. Most of the modifications were out of sight, yet surprisingly Reliant chose to re-designate the later cars as SE6a models. Firstly the scuttle structure was beefed up around the door hinges in order to stop the 'droopy door' syndrome. A further change of spring rates was evolved and the power steering pressure was reduced to add more 'feel to the wheel' as well as extend the life of the rack seals. While no complaints about the brakes had been received, Reliant engineers felt that they were only just adequate for a car weighing 24¾cwt, particularly as they had remained unchanged since the pattern was first used on the Sabre 6, which weighed only 19¾cwt, with a similar performance. In order to find a production system which offered larger rear brake drums Reliant had to turn to Lockheed for supplies of MGB rear brake components with 10in

The Scimitar Matures

drums as opposed to the 9in Girling drums. At the front, disc diameter actually came down from 10.82in to 10.5in and there were two piston calipers in place of the three piston Girling units. Presumably Reliant engineers felt that the increased carrying capacity of the SE6 merited more rear braking power relative to the front than had been the case on the earlier cars. No external changes were made to the SE6a, which makes it even more surprising that the model number was altered. At about this time the supply of Dunlop chrome-rimmed, alloy-centred composite wheels dried up and Wolfrace 6in × 14in all alloy wheels entered the price list as an optional extra in their place. The inelegant fibreglass plain wheel trims pierced with a ring of small holes remained as standard equipment. The tyres were the same 185 × 14 section for both types of wheel, as had been the case since the GTE was introduced in 1968.

Wolfrace alloy wheels became an optional extra in 1977 for the SE6a.

Predictably the SE6a was not radically different from the SE6 and apart from detailed visual inspection of the brake master cylinder there was little to tell the two models apart. The revisions included were the sort that would have entered the specification by the usual course of development without any announcement under normal conditions. Perhaps Reliant wanted to emphasise, to dealers in particular, that the latest GTE was now fully developed and that, hopefully, most of the teething troubles had now been eliminated. The SE6 was not only aiming up-market in appeal, but its price was rising to such an extent that it had to sell on its merits against mass-produced rivals, which were often cheaper. However, the Scimitar always had a distinctive appearance and the promise of a long life on its side and it was still no mean performer, as the 'Autocar' road test figures portray:

	SE6a	Capri 3000 (A)	Lancia HPE	Datsun 260Z
Capacity (cc)	2,994	2,994	1,995	2,565
Power (bhp)	135	138	119	150
Max speed (mph)	118	114	116	120
0-60mph (sec)	9.4	10.1	10.6	9.9
mpg	21.2	20.9	20.3	23.9
Weight (lb)	2,770	2,580	2,400	2,630
Price (£)	5,891	4,744	4,882	6,501

The Scimitar floorpan and outer shell were moulded on one rotating jig.

The Scimitar Matures

The Volvo P1800ES had now disappeared from their model lists, but the Lancia HPE series was another continental newcomer to follow the GTE theme quite closely, even though its twin cam power unit was only two thirds of the size of the Ford engine. The construction of the SE6a was clearly not the most weight conscious, neither were its aerodynamics outstanding, but it acquitted itself very well against comparable machines in 1977. However its handling was now far from sporting and it no longer appealed to the enthusiastic driver, whom Reliant had chosen to abandon in favour of the more mature owner. Since the GTE was now competing with Jaguar, BMW and Mercedes in certain markets and was sold alongside them occasionally, its lack of development and build quality tended to be accentuated.

Certainly the quality of the bodywork was far better than that of the late SE5a cars, probably because the fresh mouldings were cured more slowly at ambient temperature rather than passing through the low baking process. Although the basic assembly sequence was similar to that used for the previous model, greater care and inspection were introduced to reduce the warranty claims and grumbles from the dealers.

SE6 bodyshells curing outside the Kettlebrook factory.

During 1977, the Hodge Group sold its 76% share in the Reliant Motor Company to Nash Securities of Kettering, handing control of the group to Mr J. F. Nash, for a price of 1½p per share or £375,000. This was particularly surprising as a consortium of four businessmen, namely John Barber of BL, Donald Healey, Tony Good of Jensen and Joseph Beherman from Belgium, had previously offered 2p per share only to have it rejected. Following closely after these moves, in December 1977, a surprising upheaval in the Reliant Board resulted in the resignation of Ray Wiggin, who was replaced by Ritchie Spencer. Mr. Spencer had only joined Reliant in August 1976 as Personnel Director, having held a similar position in the shipbuilding industry prior to his move to Tamworth. There were clearly differences within the Board about Ray Wiggin's ambitious plans for the future and concern over existing stocks and manning levels within the company. The Scimitar was not selling as well as had been hoped and profits reflected this fact, so it was felt some pruning within Reliant was necessary. One of Ritchie Spencer's first tasks was the distasteful one of announcing redundancies and cutbacks to restore the balance sheets to a healthier state.

Under the new management, the SE6a continued in production at a reduced rate with no further development, until in 1980 Ford abandoned production of the venerable 3-litre V6 Essex engine in favour of the Cologne designed and built 2.8-litre V6. Reliant had little option, but to adapt the GTE where necessary to accept this lighter and slightly more compact power unit. While the maximum power developed by the German engine was similar to the obsolete 3-litre, at 135bhp at about the same rpm, the maximum torque of 159ft lb at 3,000rpm was well down on the 172ft lb at 3,000rpm produced by the Essex engine. To counter this, Reliant reduced the rear axle ratio of the GTE from 3.31:1 to 3.54:1 in order to maintain performance levels. Some installation problems were encountered, particularly as the distributor of the new engine was at the back of the block causing it to be embedded in the Scimitar bulkhead. Reliant equipped the engine with an electronic ignition system to avoid the need to service the distributor, which would have been a very tiresome process. For space reasons, they could only utilise the carburettor version of the Ford unit although they allocated space at the left-hand front corner of the engine compartment to accommodate some of the relevant fuel injection hardware should customers demand it. Meanwhile the battery was moved back alongside the engine itself, which no doubt helped weight distribution slightly, as did the lighter engine block. Reliant wisely re-designed the cooling system to incorporate a separate pressurised header tank, as on the SE4a and SE5 models and at a stroke eliminated the cooling problems of the SE6a. For cost reasons Reliant did not employ the new 5 speed gearbox that Ford used with this new engine in the Granada, which

The Scimitar Matures

would have been a vast improvement over the clumsy gearchange of the old Capri box, which was retained and needed a special bellhousing.

Cosmetically the revised Scimitar, now termed the SE6b, received a simplified frontal treatment, devoid of any lettering or chrome strip between the headlights, just a single shield-shape badge in the centre of an enlarged black plastic grille. A more pronounced 'chin-type' spoiler moulded into the front apron was barely noticeable and was intended to improve straightline stability. Moulded rubber side strips were glued to the sides of the bodywork and doors to offer more protection and emphasise the existing moulded rib. Two-tone paint schemes were introduced, using a lighter colour to form a broad band along the sides in line with the top half of the wheel arches.

The SE6b was distinguished by a deeper front grille and side rubbing strips.

The SE6b was now some 50lb lighter than its predecessor, mainly at the front, so spring and damper rates at this end were changed once more giving a slight improvement in handling. While the performance figures were almost identical on paper, the manner in which they were achieved differed considerably. The new engine needed to be revved to higher levels and more use had to be made of the gearbox to keep up with the more relaxed performance produced by the 3-litre cars. Noise levels increased in consequence, causing some long-standing Scimitar owners to regret the passing of the old engine, which had suited the characteristics of the GTE so well. Confirmation of this feeling is illustrated by Ritchie Spencer insisting on having the 3-litre engine in his own Scimitars after the introduction of the 2.8-litre version.

Since the debut of the SE6b coincided with the birth of the Scimitar convertible, some of the extra scuttle stiffening built into that bodyshell was also incorporated in the GTE. This involved a tubular steel hoop which was anchored to the central transmission tunnel behind the facia in an attempt to reduce scuttle shake in the open model. The SE6b benefited too, in that the car felt rather more taut than the SE6/6a.

The SE6/6a front grille incorporated a polished name bar and bonnet badge.

The Scimitar Matures

In order to improve the driver's lot as well as the showroom appeal of the Scimitar, new additions were included in the specification such as an intermittent wash/wipe facility and electrically operated mirrors. New upholstery materials and colours, including black, chocolate and mushroom, became available. The seat coverings were made of a crushed velvet type of nylon velour which gave an impression of greater opulence to the interior.

In retrospect, Reliant possibly did not develop the Scimitar enough at the point where they had to fit the new Ford engine. Apart from the omission of the 5 speed gear box and fuel injection, the absence of air conditioning and electric sunroof was noticeable when comparing competitive models in the £11,000 price bracket in which the Scimitar found itself. However, one belated feature on which the company must be commended was the galvanising applied to all chassis in the Reliant range from 1981, which endowed the Scimitar in particular with the longest life potential of almost any car in production anywhere in the world.

The SE6b had a deeper grille with no letters and a single large motif.

Unfortunately, the industrial recession which descended on Britain in 1981 nullified all efforts to promote sales, which suddenly plummeted downwards. Production was now centred on the ground floor of the Old Mill building at Two Gates and only a handful of experienced craftsmen, producing two to three cars a week, were employed. This state of affairs continued for another four years before it was rumoured in 1985 that the Scimitar was to be axed. Repeated protests by frustrated dealers persuaded Reliant to extend the life of the car by producing only to order. This hand-to-mouth situation continued until November 1986 when the last GTE left the line, destined to be Princess Anne's seventh and final Scimitar and her first with power-assisted steering. On that regal note Reliant's flagship was removed from the company's price list without any replacement of a similar nature, only a common name. The Patrick Motor Group acquired a zero mileage GTE for their collection, which should present Reliant with a few warranty claims!

Note the hand-stitched leatherwork in the rear of this specially built SE6a.

Undoubtedly the GTE could have remained in production at the rate of 100-150 per annum for many more years, as the residual order book of 30 suggests, but that level did not, unfortunately, fit in with Reliant's plans. Also, supplies of many of the components, such as seats, door furniture and control switches, purchased from outside sources presented increasing problems as numbers diminished and their use in other applications ceased through obsolescence. Equally, much of the trim was manufactured by moulding and extrusion processes, which are only economic when hundreds of examples are required. To continue production with unaltered specification would have demanded uneconomic levels of stockholding. Furthermore, as production dropped, smaller companies were employed to manufacture specific components for the Scimitar. Many of these concerns were themselves casualties of the recession, causing the supplies of certain parts to dry up suddenly and the associated tooling was either destroyed or proved too expensive for Reliant to purchase. Much re-engineering would have been necessary to allow more modern fittings to be used and Reliant felt that such development was just not viable and they had little option, but to allow their most famous product to fade away.

Scimitars have always been hand-built cars as is evident here.

It is an amazing coincidence that the Ford Capri, perhaps the nearest mass-produced competitor to the GTE, was launched one month after the introduction of the Scimitar and the last 2.8 Capri left the Cologne production line one month after the last 2.8-litre SE6B left Two Gates destined for Royal hands. Total Capri production including all engine variation amounted to 1,886,647 which rather dwarfs the 15,273 SE5 & SE6 Scimitars made. Both models represented an era of individual sporting cars whose place has largely been taken by highly modified production saloons.

In June 1987 Middlebridge Engineering negotiated to buy the production rights of the GTE and GTC from Reliant together with the drawings, technical data, body moulds, assembly jigs and Scimitar trademark for £400,000. This followed earlier unsuccessful attempts by Peter Boam and John McAuley to raise capital for the same purpose. They approached Middlebridge Engineering headed by Robin Hamilton, former manager of the Nimrod Aston Martin racing team, which lead to the successful negotiations and they will hold directorships in the new venture. The new owners hope to commence production later in 1987 at the rate of 75 per year rising to 500 per annum in three years. The cars will be powered by the latest Ford V6 2.9-litre engine and 5 speed gearbox and a higher level of hand-made fittings will be included in the specification leading to a rather higher asking price no doubt. However it is appropriate to state that "The Scimitar is dead. Long live the Scimitar".

Standard wheel trims of the last Scimitars were the same as fitted to the SE5a.

Drophead alternative

The Opening of a Great Estate

Scene stealers from Scimitar. The exciting new four seater convertible, the GTC, now stands alongside the re-engined GTE. Proud examples of British handbuilt high performance cars. Sophisticated and versatile, both models are available with a wide range of colours and specifications to suit individual tastes. 2.8-litre V6. 135 bhp. Around 120 mph. Price: GTE from £10,324. GTC from £11,360 includes VAT and Car Tax (delivery and plates extra).

SCIMITAR

CHAPTER 7

Drophead alternative

AS WE HAVE seen the SE6/6a never sold as well as its predecessor and after reaching a peak of 1,600 cars sold in 1977 production was reduced drastically over the next four years to a mere trickle of three cars a week in 1982. The main reasons why this model never quite came up to expectations must be the initial teething troubles, necessitating a number of design revisions and the increasingly critical area of the market the GTE now occupied. The Scimitar was now competing against more prestigious and better developed cars, with which it did not always compare favourably, although it definitely had versatility and a distinctive quality in its appearance. Reliant badly needed to produce a car which again filled a vacant space in the range offered by the larger manufacturers, as had the first GTE back in 1968.

Glancing through the lists of cars being produced in the late 1970s, the absence of soft top convertibles becomes apparent, apart from a few specialists such as Morgan and Bristol. BL had axed the MGB and Midget while the open Triumph TR6 and Spitfire were about to go, albeit to be replaced briefly by the unloved TR7. The last open Jaguar was made in 1975 and the Triumph Stag was also doomed, for cost and warranty reasons. Ritchie Spencer was aware of the paucity of open cars, whose manufacturers had been frightened off largely by the proposed safety regulations in the main USA export market. This factor was irrelevant to Reliant, whose last foray in that field was in 1962 with the introduction of their first four wheeled convertible, the Sabra. The separate chassis construction of the Scimitar lent itself more than most passenger vehicles to the topless format and it was not difficult to visualise the GTE in such a guise offering four seats as well. Since the four seater Triumph Stag was virtually extinct, the nearest competitor with a similar layout was the Lancia Beta Spider 2000, which was both smaller and cheaper than the Stag. The Mercedes SLC was of comparable size but had a price tag of £20,000 in 1977. Reliant assessed that the potential UK market for open GT cars was between 2,000-2,500 per annum and very much in line with their production capability.

Model	Price Nov. '77	UK Sales Jan-Oct '76	Jan-Oct '77
Triumph Stag	£6,908	1,838	1,484
Beta Spider	£4,884	—	307
Scimitar GTE	£6,332	737	1,188
Estimated Open GT sales for 12 months		2,200	2,500

Thus the Reliant Board approached Ogle Design to re-work the rear half of the SE6 bodyshape into a four seater convertible, while retaining as much of the original panels and fittings as possible, for obvious cost and development reasons. Tom Karen of Ogle responded eagerly to this new challenge and quickly presented a neat adaptation of his earlier work, involving new panelwork aft of the rear wheel centres to form a separate boot compartment and lid. For structural and safety reasons it was agreed that a roll-over hoop should be retained, as on the GTE, and connecting this to the top of the windscreen rail added further potential rigidity to the bodyshell as well as giving it an integrated appearance. Quite clearly the previous design of the Stag had influenced this plan and little new ground was broken by Ogle in this instance. Minor modifications to the rear light surrounds, with the removal of the corner vent grilles and the extension of the bumper moulding to meet the rear wheel aperture, gave the bodyshape a more compact appearance with an identity of its own.

The decapitated GTE with Ogle-designed rear modifications were the basis of the Scimitar Convertible.

Drophead Alternative

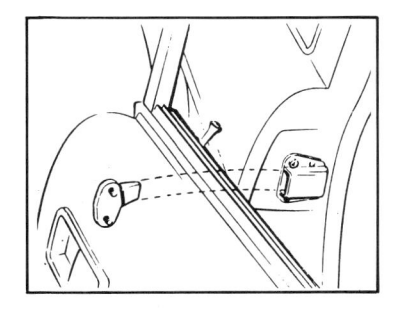

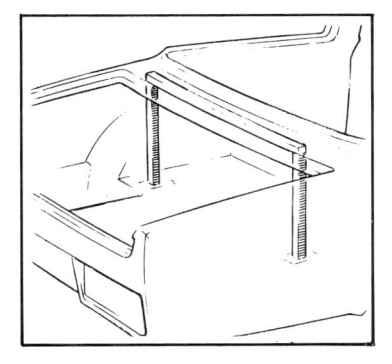

These diagrams show the strengthening applied to the door latches and boot area.

The development of this revised model was once again entrusted to Ken Wood's department. Apart from the fibreglass surgery to form the new shape, which was relatively straightforward, the main task was to restore sufficient rigidity to the bodyshell and so prevent the dreaded scuttle-shake which threatens all open cars. The extremely strong box section GTE chassis provided all the necessary beam strength, so often lacking when the roof is removed from a car using the almost universal monocoque method of construction from pressed steel. Thus there was no danger of the decapitated Scimitar sagging in the middle, but the problem of eliminating relative movement of either end of the remaining bodywork, by introducing additional torsional rigidity, was still present in this case. Reliant's team tackled this aspect by firstly bonding in a bridge structure using 1in square section tubing across the front bulkhead linking the door pillars with the central transmission tunnel behind the facia. A simpler structure straddled the gap between the rear wheel arches to prevent the hollow luggage compartment from distorting under road conditions. Further tubing was incorporated into the windscreen pillars extended down to meet the door pillars and connected via the top screen rail to the twin-tube roll-over hoop by a gussetted brace above the centre of the front passenger compartment. The roll hoop itself was modified at the top corners in that these were reversed to form concave sections to allow room for the folding hood rails to lie flat when this was erected. The doors also contributed to the overall rigidity by the fitting of a dovetail catch which consisted of a wedge-shaped tongue on the trailing edge of the door which engaged with a suitable housing on the door pillar. The hood mechanism probably gave the Development Department the biggest headache and proved to be one of the chief weaknesses in the model in the eyes of many subsequent customers.

The extra scuttle bracing and twin roll bars are clearly visible in this photo taken during body development.

Reliant had little experience of car hood design; their last attempt was in 1962 for the Sabre 4, which was intended for the hardy wind-in-the-hair brigade who were not over concerned about some ingress of moisture from inefficient hood sealing. Thus it was not surprising that a certain amount of technological poaching was considered necessary to achieve a satisfactory arrangement. What more logical model from which to gain inspiration than the Triumph Stag? So a hood from this car was acquired and used as a starting point for the new Scimitar convertible. The mechanism proved adaptable to the dimensions of the Ogle design and great efforts were made to produce a hood shape that looked appealing in the closed position, as in this country the chances are that it would be seen mainly in that form. For this reason two rear quarterlights were incorporated, unlike the Stag, to give reasonably generous all round visibility. Reliant did not attempt to manufacture the soft top themselves, but wisely contracted out this operation to the experts at the Coventry Hood Company. Highest quality German Happich material was used instead of the cheaper vinyl found in most two seater sports cars.

The hood was evolved from a Triumph Stag framework.

Drophead Alternative

These views show the excellent visibility afforded by the rear quarterlights incorporated in the hood as well as its pleasing shape.

The seating layout of the GTE was retained unaltered and the folding rear seats allowed uninterrupted access to the boot from the passenger compartment once a temporary carpeted panel was removed. This endowed the convertible with an exceptional luggage capacity for such a car, ranging from 7.2 cubic feet with four seats in use, up to double that volume with only two seats occupied. In the latter situation it was also able to accommodate skis and other long items without the need for the special boot racks sometimes devised for soft top cars. The fuel range was not impaired by the new body shape as there was still room for the 20 gallon tank under the rear compartment floor, and the filler remained in the middle of the back panel, neatly below the boot lock.

The substantial T-Bar roll cage assists body rigidity as well as protecting passengers in an accident.

Drophead Alternative

The prototype of the Scimitar convertible, termed the SE8, was finished in 1978 and registered XJW 247T, when it was powered initially by the usual Essex 3-litre V6 engine current at that time. However, the new model was not launched until March 1980, coincident with the enforced adoption by Reliant of the 2.8-litre Cologne V6 engine. The prototype was re-engineered to accept the new power unit with attendant changes to the cooling system and rear axle as applied to the revised GTE (SE6b). The car was eventually bought from the factory by Mike McCarthy, then Editor of 'Old Motor' magazine, in February 1981 with 23,000 miles on the clock. It was subsequently sold to vintage sports car racer, Martin Morris, who now uses it to tow his ERA or Jaguar D-type to race meetings here and on the Continent.

No changes were made to the front of the Scimitar when designing the GTC.

Logically the new car was called the Scimitar GTC and was known as the SE8b following the adoption of the 2.8-litre engine, which was used in all the production models. The press greeted the new drophead with statements such as a 'breath of fresh air' and a 'comforting rarity', which it certainly was, now that the late lamented Stag was conveniently obsolete. The neat bodywork was widely approved even if it did not reach quite the same levels of elegance and detail finish as the Triumph convertible. Many testers commented on the dated instrument layout and firm ride, both of which added to the almost vintage feel of the car. While it was hardly fair to compare the GTC with the Stag, which was now out of production, there was virtually no other yardstick anywhere near its asking price of £11,360 by which to judge the new Scimitar variant. This figure was several thousand pounds dearer than the final selling price of the Triumph, but inflation was taking its toll. The Scimitar definitely scored higher marks for performance, handling, economy and durability and it did not have an Achilles' heel of the scale suffered by the Stag's V8 engine which needed scrupulous maintenance to avoid calamity at quite low mileages. The Reliant needed frequent maintenance, but of a far more routine nature, to its front suspension and transmission oil levels. However most of its make up was well tested by this stage and the combination of a GRP body, galvanised steel chassis and stainless brightwork augured well for a very long life expectancy. Comparisons on paper between the Scimitar GTC, Stag and Mercedes 280SL make interesting reading:

	Scimitar GTC (Manual)	Triumph Stag (Auto)	Mercedes 280SL (Auto)
Capacity (cc)	2,792	2,997	2,746
Power (bhp)	135	146	185
Max speed (mph)	114	112	118
0-60mph (secs)	9.7	9.9	9.5
mpg (overall)	21	18.9	17.2
Weight (cwt)	26.3	24.7	30.2
Price (£)	11,360 (1980)	6,908 (1977)	17,600 (1981)

From this summary the Scimitar seems to offer very good value for money, especially as the seating capacity was more generous and the maintenance cost far lower than the Mercedes. However the hopes of Reliant that the GTC would further increase their penetration of the specialist car market were not to be fulfilled, as indeed those of British Leyland for the Stag were similarly dashed. Possibly the Scimitar drophead arrived at just the wrong time, for the British economy was on the brink of a severe recession coupled with rising oil prices. Both factors boded ill for any manufacturer of luxury goods, of which large cars were undoubtedly a prime example. This was a sad blow to Reliant, who had produced a worthy British car capable of fending off continental opposition in its particular field despite its somewhat old-fashioned features. The marque did not have the charisma to attract overseas buyers in the way Mercedes had acquired over its many years of making prestige motor cars, and was entirely dependent on the home market which turned against it now that times were harder.

A fibreglass hard top, fully trimmed with a heated rear window and vinyl roof covering was available as an optional extra after 1981 and became standard in later years to try and attract more sales all year round. It proved more successful in keeping the interior dry than did the hood when raised. Other options included power steering, Wolfrace wheels, electric mirrors, windows and aerial, but in practice few cars were built without all these features. In fact buyers had to specify manual steering if they required it in preference to the optional powered variety.

The vinyl covered hardtop was very stylish.

THE SCIMITAR AND ITS FOREBEARS

Delightful summer shot of a GTC in North Wales.

The latest Scimitar sports car in suitably modern surroundings at Birmingham University.

THE SCIMITAR AND ITS FOREBEARS

xvi

The abandoned Bertone-designed SE82 prototype in the Reliant Development Department.
The very successful Scimpart supercharged V8 GTE built and campaigned by Les Trafford seen at Silverstone.

Reliant produced 300 convertibles during 1980 and the evidence of the difficulty they had in selling these models was abundantly clear from the rows of GTCs parked outside the Two Gates factory at that time, forming a temporary landmark for travellers along that section of the A5. Even the brief acquisition of a GTC by Prince Edward did not have the same stimulating effect on its sales as that bestowed on the GTE by his sister ten years earlier. Dealers were encouraged to offer generous discounts during 1981 to try and clear stocks and Reliant slashed the production rate to just three cars during that year. Subsequently about 20 GTCs were produced each year from 1982 until the last model left the line at the end of 1986. After this bitter experience it became Ritchie Spencer's policy to produce cars strictly to orders received from the dealers. This rule has been applied to both the three- and four wheeled ranges of vehicles and has no doubt contributed to the continued existence of the company through that difficult period. Few could have foreseen the darkening clouds of industrial depression which engulfed Britain and many other countries during the early 1980s, particularly back in 1977 when the GTC was being planned. Eventually only 443 examples of this flagship of the Scimitar range were produced and now that it is obsolete it has become, not surprisingly, the most sought after model of the range, for which steadily increasing prices are asked. Even after its demise that same gap in the market remains, only partially satisfied by the growing hoards of cabriolet versions of popular hatchbacks. While many of these models offer similar performance and accommodation as the GTC, they lack the style and long-lasting features of the final Scimitar.

Prince Edward drove a GTC briefly.

DROPHEAD ALTERNATIVE

Production of the GTC ceased in November 1986 along with the GTE. Both models suffered from lack of development in their latter years, and as sales diminished so the unit cost of production rose. Added to which availability of many components was drying up as manufacturers revised the ranges of cars from which these items originated. Reliant could not afford constantly to change their cars in tune with such developments and some of the last cars made lacked bright trim round the front and side windows simply because the suppliers of these items could not continue producing the small quantities now required.

The recent acquisition of the manufacturing rights of the GTE and GTC by the Milton Keynes company, Middlebridge Engineering would indicate that these two fine cars will not now be condemned to an untimely end. Thus up-market versions of both models may soon be produced thanks to the finance put up by the president of Middlebridge, Mr. Kohli Nakauchi.

A GTC bodyshell being lowered onto its chassis on the same line as the GTE.

A shapely pair!

Visibility was still very good with the hardtop fitted.

A new young blade

THE GETAWAY CAR

The Scimitar SS1 gets you away in style. Gets you away in comfort. With crisp performance, impeccable road manners and high standards of reliability and economy.

Styled by Michelotti and built by a new technology process, the body is rustproof, knock resistant and inexpensive to repair.

And the spacious interior with its deep, velour faced seats and relaxed driving position is designed for comfort.

Power is provided by well proven 1300cc or 1600cc overhead camshaft engines. The 1600cc, shown here, achieves 110mph, 0-60 in 9.6 secs. and 46mpg at a constant 56mph. The SS1 gets you away from the humdrum.

From just a little under £7000.

SCIMITAR SS1
RELIANT · TAMWORTH · ENGLAND

CHAPTER 8

New young blade

IT WAS APPARENT to Reliant by 1978 that the tide had turned in the fortunes of the GTE, which was becoming dated in various aspects and in need of mechanical and trim revisions to revitalise its appeal. Ritchie Spencer chose to devote the company's resources into producing the convertible GTC instead, in the hope that considerable sales could be achieved by attacking a new division of the market now seemingly deserted. As we have seen this prediction was not borne out for a combination of economic and technical reasons, causing the car to be considered rather old-fashioned from the start. At about the same time Reliant were considering the possibility of entering the small sports car market which was similarly devoid of models from the larger manufacturers.

The Austin Healey Sprite and TR6 had long since disappeared, albeit the latter had been replaced by the fixed head TR7. The current MG Midget, Triumph Spitfire and Fiat X19 were nearing the end of their production life without any planned replacements. Based on sales of open cars in Britain during 1976 and 1977, Reliant estimated a market of around 7,500 small 'fun' sports cars during the early 1980s.

	Price Nov 1977	UK Sales Jan-Nov '76	Jan-Nov '77
Midget	£2,221	2,299	3,551
Spitfire	£2,550	2,849	3,129
Fiat X19	£3,627	—	1,734
MGB	£3,024	1,388	1,916
10 month totals	... ...	6,536	10,330
Est. 12 month sales	... ...	7,800	12,000

These ideas were probably not unconnected with the arrival of Ed Osmond as Director of Engineering, fresh from a similar post with Triumph. His experience with open cars and the Italian designer Michelotti, who had produced so many of the body shapes for Triumph, such as the 2000, Herald and Spitfire, influenced Reliant's decision to follow the same path. Other factors leading to this move were the feeling that Michelotti had more experience than Ogle in designing open sports cars and the fact that he was a great deal cheaper than Bertone whom Reliant had already approached for designs for a GTE successor, described in the next chapter. The first design presented by Michelotti, which now adorns the Reliant Board room wall, was dated 11th December 1978.

Coincident with these moves, but quite innocent of them, a freelance designer Tony Stevens had devised a very stylish open two seater based on Reliant Kitten chassis and running gear and clothed in a fibreglass body not unlike the Lotus Elan. Tony called his creation the Cipher, which was constructed of separate bolt-on GRP panels attached to a tubular steel base frame mounted on a lowered and widened Kitten chassis. A similar principle was used, with steel panels, on the Rover 2000 (P6) and with fibreglass panels on the current Renault Espace. The motive for this design was to reduce the cost of constructing large and complicated moulds as well as appeasing insurance companies by offering smaller repair and replacement charges. Mechanically, the Cipher employed the standard Reliant 850cc 40bhp all alloy engine mated to the Kitten gearbox and a live rear axle suspended on leaf springs, while the front suspension was the standard Kitten wishbone and coil spring arrangement. The choice of Reliant products in the first place was not just because they were British and available, but because of Reliant's commitments abroad, for with the supply of Kitten parts to India for the Dolphin and to Greece for the Fox, they were unlikely to change these designs rapidly thus endangering his project.

Complicated tubular Cipher chassis based on the Kitten running gear.

A New Young Blade

The elegant Cipher body design, reminiscent of the Lotus Elan.

Unquestionably the body shape of the Cipher was, and still is, just right and does not appear dated some nine years later. Tony Stevens approached Reliant about the possibility of producing his design and they responded by producing two prototypes at Two Gates for evaluation as a production model. Following this exercise the work force were very enthusiastic and the unions were all for the idea of producing the Cipher even though it was an outside design. However, the management found that it would cost in the region of £¼ million in development costs to make the Cipher a production possibility and Tony did not have these sort of resources. This was particularly sad as when the press road tested a prototype they were overwhelmingly enthusiastic about its performance and economy as well as its ride and handling. There were criticisms concerning the internal finish and rear suspension behaviour, but these were to be expected of projects at this stage and could have been remedied quite easily before production took place.

Unfortunately, Reliant were not prepared to contribute financially to any development of Cipher, even though they approved of its concept and agreed to build it in principle. Ritchie Spencer made it quite clear to Tony Stevens at one of their meetings that they were considering production of a Reliant sports car using a Michelotti design, which was obviously the reason behind their reluctance to give additional support to the Cipher despite the possible extra outlet for the Reliant produced running gear. The company also considered they needed a more powerful car than the Cipher to fill the gap left in the sports car market and Ford units were planned for the new Reliant, in line with the Scimitar. Thus Tony was left to his own devices to find a backer for his potentially very successful car which he has not so far succeeded in doing, even though he has re-engineered it to accept Renault running gear to make it more attractive internationally.

The body sections used to produce the Cipher.

A New Young Blade

Prior to adopting the Michelotti design, Reliant had also considered making the Equus two seater shown by Vauxhall at the Motor Show as a futuristic project using General Motors mechanicals, but no satisfactory scheme could be drawn up for such a co-operative venture. Sadly, Michelotti, or 'Micho' as he became known at Tamworth, died before the details were finalised for the commissioned design. However Ritchie Spencer and his Board members approved the latest presentation for the body shape and it was then Ed Osmond's responsibility to make it a production feasibility. From the outset he was determined to use pressed plastic panels, produced by less labour intensive means, which could be bolted to the chassis, as determined for the Cipher. Which came first is a matter of conjecture, but certainly Tony Stevens had no knowledge of the Michelotti design until he had already constructed one of his own cars. The use of separate panels involved introducing more shut lines in the bodywork than Michelotti had intended, resulting in a far less attractive appearance. This form of construction also ruled out the use of a simple ladder chassis, as on the GTE with its integral bodyshell. A sub-structure was now necessary to support the panels as well as providing anchorages for door hinges, latches and safety belts. A basic backbone chassis was evolved with welded tubular outriggers braced to the central backbone by triangulated pressed steel plates.

The excellent backbone chassis of the SS1.

The suspension was now very much state of the art, comprising double wishbone and coil springs at the front controlled by almost horizontal telescopic dampers acting between vertical abutments on each top wishbone and a central pivot on the chassis in front of the engine. The rear suspension was also independent, with coil springs and trailing arms lifted straight from the Ford Sierra, but naturally with different spring and damper settings. The unbroken loyalty to Ford power units and transmissions was maintained in this new small car by the use of the 1300cc and 1600cc CVH engines, which were mounted in-line and mated to the Sierra 4 or 5 speed gearbox behind them in traditional sports car fashion. Only carburettor versions of these engines were employed as there was insufficient vertical room for the fuel injection equipment. This omission deprived the new car of some much needed performance in face of competition from the increasing number of 'hot hatchbacks', which in most cases were faster as well as more spacious and comfortable. One feature which was inherited from the GTE was the positioning of the spare wheel, ahead of the engine and behind the cross-flow radiator.

This cutaway diagram shows the all independent suspension, in particular the interesting front damper mounting.

A New Young Blade

The facia incorporates Metro instruments in a well designed layout.

The interior was designed by Jevon Thorpe, a graduate aged 25 from Lanchester Polytechnic, who co-ordinated a range of instruments and switches from the Metro with Escort control stalks and seats from the TR7 into a simple modern layout, finished in pleasing colours and materials. Apart from the cockpit structure, only the steering wheel and the cranked gear lever were of Reliant manufacture. The body panel construction broke new ground for Reliant as only the floorpan, doors and boot lining were made from the traditional hand laid-up fibreglass at which the company were possibly the most experienced in the automotive field. The front and rear sections, together with the wings and doors, were manufactured by the Dunlop group from reinforced reaction injection moulded plastic (RRIM). The resulting panels were soft and deformable, similar to those used on the Porsche 928 rear end and many of the American 'friendly fenders'. The boot lid was formed by cold pressing impregnated fibreglass matting for 20 minute cycles, as already used to produce the doors for the GTE and three-wheelers. The bonnet of the new sports car was too large and complicated to undergo this process so Reliant copied Lotus in making this component by vacuum-assisted resin injection moulding. This involves gel-coating the female mould with resin which is then filled with continuous filament fibreglass matt encasing a core of closed cell rigid urethane. The metal bonnet hinge fixings are now located, after which the mould is closed and about 14kg of catalysed resin is injected at one end while a vacuum is applied at the other end to suck the resin throughout the whole area of the panel until it overflows around the edges. After about ten minutes curing the bonnet is removed from the mould, trimmed, and is ready for painting.

The speed of producing the various panels from different materials and processes could not be matched by the assembly teams, who found that the fit of these components was far from accurate due to the differing shrinkage tolerances displayed by each process. Furthermore the chassis was manufactured in West Germany and proved to have variations in dimension due to its complicated structure. Thus the Two Gates production line were faced with the problem of making the panels fit each individual chassis by means of grinding and re-drilling where necessary. This in turn made assembly both slower and far more expensive than expected.

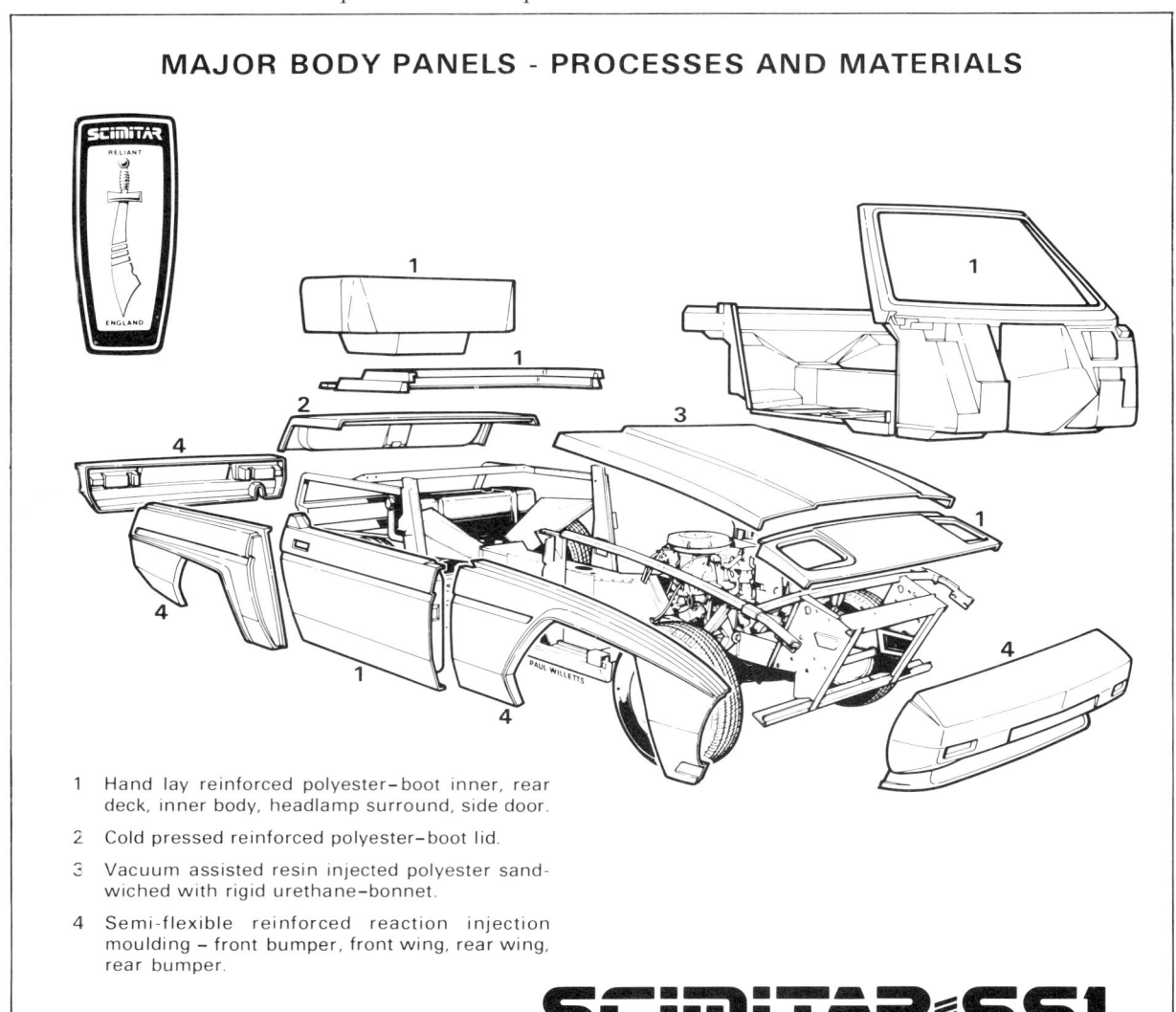

MAJOR BODY PANELS - PROCESSES AND MATERIALS

1. Hand lay reinforced polyester — boot inner, rear deck, inner body, headlamp surround, side door.
2. Cold pressed reinforced polyester — boot lid.
3. Vacuum assisted resin injected polyester sandwiched with rigid urethane — bonnet.
4. Semi-flexible reinforced reaction injection moulding — front bumper, front wing, rear wing, rear bumper.

SCIMITAR SS1
RELIANT · TAMWORTH · ENGLAND

A New Young Blade

The new Reliant was launched at the 1984 Motor Show at the NEC as the Scimitar SS1 and was displayed in pearlescent white alongside the last of the GTE models in a similar finish. There can be little doubt that the Reliant stand was among the busiest at the show that year as queues of eager youngsters were ushered, in limited numbers at a time, to inspect the car on its raised dias. Sadly interest was tinged with doubt concerning the appearance of the new small Scimitar whose profile was awkward and messy in places due to the numerous panel joints, which were none too accurate for the reasons already mentioned. Nevertheless the press road testers were very complimentary about the chassis behaviour of the SS1 even though its performance and panel fit were not impressive. The 1300 model was really quite slow, but the larger-engined car was reasonably competitive, as the figures below illustrate:

This view emphasises the abrupt windscreen angle and curious wheel arch mouldings.

	SS1 (1600)	Fiat X19	Morgan 4/4	Caterham Super 7
Capacity (cc)	1,596	1,498	1,596	1,599
Power (bhp)	96	85	96	130
Max speed (mph)	108	110	110	109
0-60mph (secs)	11.5	10.8	13.4	6.0
mpg (overall)	32.8	26.8	28	25
Price (£)	7,999	7,107	9,300	8,512

In such company the Fiat scores highest on price, looks and handling; the Morgan on charisma and investment potential; the Caterham on sheer performance. Economy and durability of its bodywork appear to be the only factors favouring Reliant's new baby,

The profile of the SS1 was the most favourable angle to view the car.

A New Young Blade

but even these could not overcome the strong reservations most people expressed about its looks. This latter quality is of prime importance in a sports car, which by its nature is an indulgence for most buyers and a status symbol for some owners. The slot in the market was undoubtedly present and the price of the SS1 was about right, but the disappointing sales of 500 in 1985 and only 300 in 1986 against the projected 2,000 per annum must be largely attributed to its controversial lines and build quality. Even Ritchie Spencer was reported to have admitted that the styling was weak at the front and not to everyone's taste. 'Performance Car' magazine summed up the small Scimitar as the 'missed opportunity of the decade', while 'Car' journalists liked the car immensely from the driving seat, but confessed it was no treat to the eye and should be re-styled before it was too late.

Certain aspects of the SS1 remind one of the original Sabre 4.

When Reliant produced the Sabre 4, which received very similar comments, they were able to modify the bodywork quite quickly and cheaply within their own factory. In the case of the SS1, Reliant found themselves in a far less favourable position to incorporate any revisions of a major nature. With most of the car being manufactured by outside concerns, some of them abroad, it was not easy to cancel contracts or change components quickly. Thus they were stuck with the situation of producing a car which honestly looked to be cheap for the price, but was very expensive to make — just the opposite of the ideal manufacturing policy so skilfully achieved by the Ford Motor Company. Tragically the chassis and suspension of the car were excellent and if only customers could have been persuaded actually to drive the SS1 then probably more of them would have taken out their cheque books and Watermans with which to sign them. A stylish fibreglass hardtop was added to the list of options in late 1985, which extended the versatility of the car, but did not in itself generate increased sales.

Even though the company could do little to alter the car's appearance in the short term they did respond to the demand for more performance, not by boosting the power of the existing Ford engines, but by inserting the Nissan Silvia 1800 Turbo engine instead. The reasons for this apparently strange move were two-fold. Firstly there was not room for the fuel injection and turbochargers fitted to the Ford unit and secondly it would not pass the American emission laws, which would have prevented any possibility of exporting the

The hardtop has a pleasant shape which improves the appearance of the car when fitted.

A New Young Blade

SS1. The Nissan engine not only fitted the engine bay beautifully, but had also passed the emission requirements for the USA. The boost in power, price and performance was considerable and the 1800ti, as it was called, now came into competition with the highly respected Toyota MR2 mid-engined sports car. The small Scimitar could now hold its own in the performance stakes as well as possessing very respectable roadholding qualities.

	Scimitar 1800ti	Toyota MR2
Capacity (cc)	1,809	1,600
Power (bhp)	135	122
Max speed (mph)	126	120
0-60mph (secs)	6.9	7.9
mpg (overall)	27.6	27.5
Weight (lb)	1,940	2,350
Price (£)	10,300	11,999

It is staggering to note how nearly the price of the 1800ti was approaching that of the GTE, which perhaps indicates what a bargain the latter car was at the end of its life. The only distinguishing features denoting the uprated Scimitar sports car from its smaller

The front and rear spoilers plus roll-bar distinguish the 1800Ti.

engined brethren were a black rubber spoiler on the boot lid and standard alloy wheels. One change underneath the lack-lustre bodywork, apart from the Garrett turbocharged engine, was a chassis now galvanised like the larger Scimitars. This process was applied to all the two seaters after chassis no. 900 and simultaneously the title SS1 was diplomatically dropped as preparations were made to launch the car in Europe. Similar plans to export the car to the United States were thwarted by the prohibitive insurance premium covering product liability.

The enhanced performance of the 1800ti produced a much needed upturn in sales, and production level at the beginning of 1987 was running at 15 per week, which should improve as spring and summer weather persuades more people to reconsider open air motoring. There can be little doubt that the one factor which would probably improve sales dramatically is a re-skin for the bodywork, or at the very least a considerable facelift. Following the demise of the GTE and GTC, Reliant should now be able to concentrate all their resources into making the small Scimitar a success, a quality which seems to have eluded all the company's open cars to date for reasons of shape or timing. The first example, the Sabre 4, achieved 208 sales in 1962/3, while more recently the GTC doubled that figure with 443, which has already been doubled again by the SS1 series. Fortunately, three-wheeler sales remain healthy and outside contracts continue to be won, giving Reliant the necessary support while the latest Scimitar matures hopefully into a winner on the scale of the GTE in the 1970s. Such hope seems unlikely to be fulfilled judging from the sales of only 100 cars during the first half of 1987.

Ritchie Spencer left Reliant for pastures new in the GKN organisation in May 1987 to be succeeded by Cyril Burton who was already a Board member. Coincidental with this management change, Reliant were reported to be seeking US aid for marketing the SS1 in America or even transferring the project completely across the Atlantic with the subsequent sale of the modern Two Gates factory site. Remaining three-wheeler production would presumably then be continued at the Kettlebrook Works alongside the body moulding lines. Such a development would seem to signal the end of all Scimitar production in this country, leaving the sports two-seater market almost vacant once more. Many are still convinced that a well styled sports car as well as an up-dated GTE could have been leaving the Tamworth factory in satisfactory numbers to keep all the factories fully occupied in the late eighties had different decisions been made ten years previously. Certainly the enthusiasm for the product and the flair to produce attractive sporting cars to fill the gaps in the market left by the major manufacturers seemed to wane over the last decade.

What might have been

Bertone studies for GTE replacement.

Ogle interpretations of possible GTE replacements in 1977.

CHAPTER 9

What might have been

EVERY CAR MANUFACTURER develops almost as many project car designs that are not pursued, as those that eventually reach production. Reliant has been no exception to this rule and fortunately some of these lost causes have escaped the bounds of the factory into private hands. Although not directly related to the development of the Scimitar, two experimental cars based on the 850cc range could have had a dramatic effect on the history of the company if they had gone beyond the prototype stage.

Soon after Ogle Design had completed the GTE they turned their attention to the possibility of extending the economy range of Reliants to include a sporting variant. In 1969 Tom Karen presented a very advanced wedge-shaped bodyshell to accommodate a mid-engined layout. John Crosthwaite meantime organised the construction of a backbone chassis, utilising 6in diameter tubing for the main members, which was to be fitted with a twin carburettor 850cc Reliant engine in-line behind the driver, but ahead of the rear axle, pointing aft. Drive from the forward-mounted gearbox was taken downwards by Hi-Vo chain to a propshaft linked to the live rear axle. The latter was located by very long radius arms with an 'A' bracket to control lateral movement, as used eventually on the Bond Bug. One running example was built, known as the FW7, and its design anticipated the

The front view of the FW7 reminds one of the much later Lotus Esprit.

successful Fiat X19 and the bodyshape, sadly unsung, fore-shadowed the Lotus Esprit and many Italian mid-engined cars. Indeed it may have inspired the Harris Mann conceived front-engined TR7, whose profile was very similar, some six years later. The cost of such a revolutionary design, coupled with its limited performance, cast doubts at Reliant about its viability. Some 16 years later the Michelotti design chosen by Reliant for the recent SS1 actually looks more dated than the brilliant FW7 prototype, no longer in existence.

Much less dramatic, and far more probable, was the Reliant evolution of the Bond Equipe, which might have entered the price list as a junior Scimitar. Still using the 2-litre Triumph chassis and running gear, Ken Wood and his bodywork development team produced moulds for a revised one-piece fibreglass bodyshell instead of the mixture of Bond and Triumph panels used in the original car, which was inherited by Reliant when they acquired Bond Cars in 1969. Although closely related to the quite good looking Bond design, it had a far more professional appearance and was apparently more rigid as a result of employing unitary construction of the type in which Reliant were undoubted experts. The success of the GTE probably contributed as much as other considerations to the disappearance of the Equipe and its proposed successor, as Reliant had

From the side the proposed FW7 anticipated the Fiat X19 shape.

WHAT MIGHT HAVE BEEN

Two views of the Reliant revamp of the Bond Equipe which never reached production.

only enough production capacity to satisfy the growing market for the new Scimitar. As mentioned in Chapter One, the Bond name was continued on the Bug for several more years even though this fascinating fun vehicle never came up to expectations from the sales angle. An extraordinary four-wheeled version, FW9, was constructed employing a tubular beam front axle located in the same way as the rear one by radius arms and lateral 'A' bracket. John Crosthwaite well remembers its go-kart-like abilities and considered it a far better proposition than its three-wheeled counterpart, but clearly his opinion was not shared in the Two Gates Board room.

Among the Sabre models, only the racing Sabre 6 (876 HWD) qualifies for listing as a unique prototype. This was a competition development of the production car intended to publicise the parent model in the motorsport scene, at which it was only partially successful. One or two variations were applied to the Scimitar Coupé, including chassis no. SC400007, which was equipped with the same independent rear suspension arrangement as the racing Sabre. The most famous Reliant prototype, albeit not actually produced by the Tamworth concern, was the Ogle GTS (Glazing Triplex Special) built by Ogle on a commission from Triplex and subsequently used by HRH The Duke of Edinburgh before being displayed to this day in the National Motor Museum in Beaulieu. A far less famous Reliant variant of the Scimitar Coupé was conceived at the factory in 1970, after the introduction of the SE5 and used some features of the latter model in an attempt to update the smaller car. This was based on a shortened GTE chassis on which was mounted a Coupé body fitted with SE5 front panel and rear light units. The wider track necessitated

Rear view of the Coupé/GTE hybrid shows SE5 rear lights and wheel arches.

modified rear wheel arches and the front mounted spare wheel and under-floor fuel tank at the rear were incorporated from the later car. This unique car, originally termed the SE6, was registered ARF 109D and was equipped with automatic transmission as it was intended for use by John Crosthwaite's wife, who only had experience with this type of gearbox, having learned to drive in the USA. For some reason the car was known as the 'Batmobile' at Reliant, before being sold by the company to a doctor. The appearance of this interesting car was an improvement over the original Ogle Daimler shape used for the production Coupés, but again the popularity of the GTE precluded the possibility of production for capacity reasons. Clearly the GTE was still far more practical as an everyday car, despite the improved luggage room of the Coupé-GTE hybrid which could still only carry two adults and two very small children in comfort.

Apart from the prototype of the SE5 utilising an extended Coupé chassis and now fitted with a Ford V8 engine, the most significant variation made by Reliant of this successful model was a four-wheel drive version. Although it was not intended for production, but was more an indulgence of the Engineering Department, such a project would be most relevant today now that all-wheel transmission is so much in vogue. However, back in 1972 Tony Rolt of Ferguson had so impressed Reliant engineers with his system that a design for an adapted GTE was drawn up by draughtsman Ted Leban with the assistance of Ossy Webb from Ferguson. In this case the torque-split of 40/60 front/rear was chosen and the drive to the front differential was taken from the rear of a special overdrive gearbox by Hi-Vo chain and propshaft containing two constant-velocity joints. An additional

The front panel from the SE5 suited the Coupé bodyshell.

advanced feature was a Dunlop Maxaret anti-locking brake system, as used eventually on the Jensen Interceptor FF. This car was registered MRF 519L, but became rather an orphan within the company, which was pre-occupied at the time developing the Robin (TW8). John Crosthwaite, who had been its main advocate, left Reliant soon afterwards to join George Turnbull in setting up the Hyundai Car Company in South Korea. On his return after two years abroad, John visited the factory to purchase a Robin for his wife and found the GTE 4 × 4, full of water and mildew, languishing behind the Development Department. He persuaded Ray Wiggin to sell the car, which John proceeded to renovate and he enjoyed four years of fascinating ownership using it as a tow car for his boating expeditions. He sold it eventually to a collector in Cheshire, where this intriguing car still resides.

Following the arrival of the production SE6, as opposed to the former hybrid of the same denomination a forward model policy was drawn up by Barrie Wills for the Reliant Board to consider in October 1977. Apart from the suggestions for a Scimitar convertible and a small two seater sports car, which later came to fruition as the GTC and SS1, a range of vehicles based on the FW11 package was formulated. FW11 was a Bertone design which evolved from a meeting between Ray Wiggin and Barrie Wills with Bertone at the 1977 Geneva Motor Show where the SE6 was launched in Europe. The new project was initially intended to replace the ageing Anadol developed by Reliant for Turkey. Derek Peck undertook the engineering of the FW11 which featured all independent suspension and was capable of accepting the full range of Ford engines from 1,300cc to 2.8-litre V6 just announced. The range of cars now envisaged is shown in the table below:

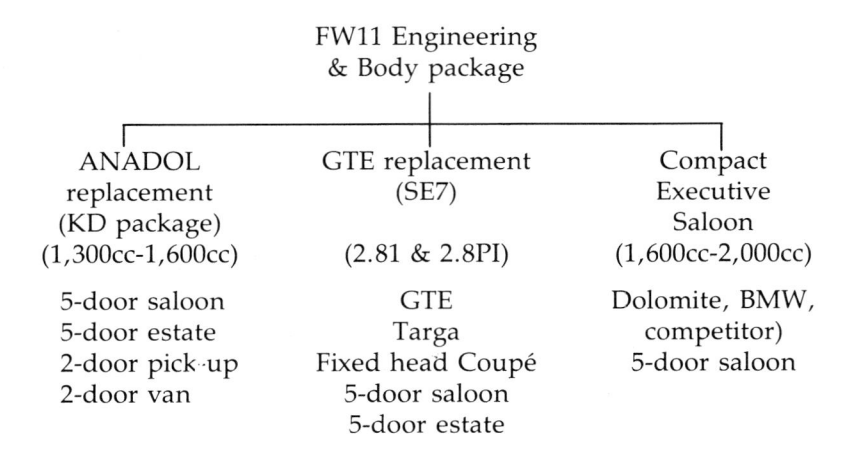

FW11 Engineering & Body package

ANADOL replacement (KD package) (1,300cc-1,600cc)	GTE replacement (SE7) (2.8I & 2.8PI)	Compact Executive Saloon (1,600cc-2,000cc)
5-door saloon	GTE	Dolomite, BMW, competitor)
5-door estate	Targa	5-door saloon
2-door pick-up	Fixed head Coupé	
2-door van	5-door saloon	
	5-door estate	

What Might Have Been

187

The Bertone designed FW11 has many similarities to Chrysler Alpine and VW Passat, but only one prototype was ever made.

Two months after this plan had been presented, Ray Wiggin was persuaded to resign followed closely by Barrie Wills and Derek Peck, who was then Director of Engineering. Wiggin and Wills formed their own consultancy businesses while Peck returned to British Leyland as Director in charge of the team which jointly designed the Rover 800 series (what might have been the future of Reliant had he stayed with Wiggin?).

The new management under Ritchie Spencer discarded the Wills plan and approached Bertone once more for an alternative design to replace the GTE since the Otosan Co. in Turkey did not take up the FW11 proposal. The new Engineering Director, Ed Osmond, travelled to Turin to view the clay model for a car which Reliant hoped to introduce in 1982, hence the project number of SE82 that applied to it. Bertone's brief was to produce a spacious 2+2 sports hatch with a large glass area and approval for the final styling was given in January 1979. An all-independent chassis was designed for the car, with a 106in wheelbase (2½in longer than the SE6) featuring double wishbone front suspension and sub-frame mounted trailing arms at the rear, probably of Ford origin. However, Reliant envisaged using the Rover 3.5-litre V8 engine, breaking their loyalty to Ford units. This development coincided with the beginning of the industrial

The most exciting possibility for replacing the GTE was designed by Bertone, known as the SE82, was tragically scrapped by Reliant.

recession of the early 1980s when a new car costing in the region of £15,000 would have been increasingly difficult to sell. After spending over £100,000 on the excitingly elegant SE82 the plug was pulled on this Porsche 928 lookalike in March 1980, after a rolling fibreglass-bodied prototype had been constructed. This machine has now apparently been dismantled and disposed of, leaving only a couple of photographs to record the details of a very worthy looking new car. It seems a great pity that there are so many instances in the motor industry where such unfinished and redundant projects are wantonly destroyed, as if they were objects of shame, when many enthusiasts would probably pay money to view them if given the opportunity. Furthermore, some of these prototypes demonstrate the skills of the design and development staff within the parent company and should be displayed at suitable shows, to act as crowd pullers as well as exhibiting the forward thinking of the manufacturer concerned. British Leyland have been similarly secretive, to this day, over the fastback TR7 derivative known as the Lynx, which allegedly was far better looking than the production two seater and certainly nothing of which to be ashamed.

As a postscript to this subject, Tom Karen was invited by 'Autocar' magazine in February 1986 to present his ideas of how he felt 'his' GTE should have been developed. He offered some very firm

Ogle's interpretation of up-dating the existing GTE bodyshell in 1986.

suggestions on the detail changes he would apply to the basically sound overall shape of the bodyshell. Firstly, the four round headlights must be retained for function and distinction amid the array of rectangular and trapezoidal units now employed in most cars. A smoother, more rounded front panel would assist the aerodynamics and could be blended in with body-coloured deformable bumpers, since black rubber or chrome steel units are now unfashionable. He felt 'eyebrows' over the wheel arches, complemented by flush wheel covers, would add impact to the side view, while the rear valence should incorporate the lights and exhaust outlets to match the front. The main cabin area could be retained so that the changes would be restricted to forming new front and rear moulds.

Clearly the interior and controls required revision by employing more recent components from current manufacturers, including a higher quality moulded facia and centre console. Once again Tom Karen favoured the round analogue instruments for similar reasons as the round headlamps — visibility and character. Careful colour coding of trim materials, made from good quality cloth and vinyl, would help the showroom image of the car enormously. Slimmer seats of the correct anatomical design would offer greater comfort and release more room for passengers as well as weighing and costing less. In such a guise a new GTE could take on all its pretenders, including the Honda Aerodeck which only now incorporates so many of the features pioneered by the Scimitar 20 years ago.

The chassis and running gear are also in dire need of improvements in line with modern developments, but Reliant have proved with the SS1 that they are capable of evolving a very competent structural design, utilising suspension components from current vehicles to extremely good effect. There is no reason why similar techniques could not be applied to the larger car.

It seems unlikely that Reliant will develop a successor to their most famous product, the much admired GTE. Having shelved the exciting SE82 project, the company is now convinced that they will achieve greater profits by producing large quantities of a hopefully more popular car than small numbers of a higher-priced vehicle. The success of this policy remains to be seen, but many people within and without the confines of the Two Gates factory lament the passing of the 'Old Scimitar', as it is affectionately known, which brought fame if not fortune to its makers.

Latest developments involving the sale of the production rights of the Scimitar GTE and GTC to Middlebridge Engineering would indicate that these models are likely to re-emerge from their Milton Keynes factory in much the same form as before with minor alterations to the power train and trim materials initially.

WHAT MIGHT HAVE BEEN

The co-operation between Reliant and Autocars of Israel in the late 1950s to produce cars abroad, which had been engineered in Tamworth, led to a succession of such projects. These outside contracts were largely developed in the Middle East by Ray Wiggin following his deep interest in countries in that region. Apart from the Sabra and Anadol range of cars covered in Chapter One, Reliant also developed fibreglass bodies for Ford Transits and Ford D100 lorry cabs to be made in Turkey.

One of the most interesting contracts won by Reliant in recent years was that of building the 200 Ford RS200 Group B rally cars required to homologate the model for international rallying. The Shenstone factory, previously used for making the alloy engines and gearboxes and later used as the spares store, was taken out of mothballs to set up a production line for this exciting car. The operation, under the control of Jerry Wilmott, required an intense pace of work to meet the deadlines set by the FIA (ruling body of international motor sport) and Ford who badly needed to establish themselves in rallying again. Shift work was required for the duration of the short-lived project which no doubt provided Reliant with some much needed income during the lean period of 1985-86, as well as many headaches. Unfortunately the life of the rally supercars was soon curtailed following a number of fatal accidents involving both competitors and spectators due to the amazing performance of the cars in conditions of close proximity between man and machine.

Had events not followed this route, it is not inconveivable that a future production model based on the RS200 might have been made by Reliant. Indeed 'what might have been?'.

Ford RS200 in full rally trim in 1987.

Ford RS200 rally cars in production at the Shenstone factory in 1986.

Owner's guide

RSSOC Magazine 1972-87

CHAPTER 10

Owner's guide

THERE IS HARDLY a specialist car made and sold that has not been the subject of a club for the benefit of its owners. In most instances the cars have left their initial owners' hands by the time they become the property of enthusiasts who possibly value the abilities of the model in question more than the first owner. The Scimitar has been no exception to this rule and the Reliant Sabre & Scimitar Owners' Club was formed by a small band of owners in 1972 headed, as it is today, by Robin Rew and Roger Tipler. At that time Robin owned the ex-works Sabre sprint car (876 HWD), following several years of running a standard six-cylinder version (92 FRP) while Roger possessed the prototype Scimitar GT (AUE 38B). Both gentlemen shared an interest in motorsport and photography and it is not surprising, therefore, that from its inception the club has become competition oriented. The inaugural meeting at Silverstone in Northamptonshire was attended by two Sabre 4s, three Sabre 6s (including two works cars, 650 GUE of Roger Heron and the aforementioned 876 HWD), the prototype Scimitar GT, two V6 Scimitar Coupés and four SE5 GTEs.

Even though Reliant had made only a brief but brave foray into the competition world with their cars, the founder members of the RSSOC considered they still had potential in this direction, particularly in hill climbing and sprints. Robin and a few others went as far as racing their Sabres in Classic events with commendable success, culminating in 876 HWD winning outright the Pomeroy Trophy held at Silverstone by the VSCC in 1982. During the previous three years the club had fielded a team of six Sabres in the annual six-hour relay races without any mechanical disasters.

Richard Ward ascending Shelsley Walsh hill climb in his Straight 6 Scimitar Coupé in 1975.

Another founder member, Joe Devlin, was a regular competitor in all forms of motor sport with his venerable Sabre 6 (42 WYD). Joe also worked at Reliant for many years and proved a very valuable personality within the club when it came to offering assistance, both verbal and physical. Sadly he died while pushing his car in the snow in 1982. Tragedy struck another Sabre enthusiast, Roger Valler, the following year while pursuing his love of working on the cars. This followed his magnificent restoration of one of the ex-works Sabre 4 rally cars (42 ENX) prior to competing with it in the 1982 Golden 50 RAC Rally. Subsequently his son John has used this car in historic rallies, just as Joe's son John continues to campaign his father's car. Incredibly, all the works rally Sabres, except 649 GUE which was written off on the 1964 Monte, continue today in one form or another, even though 648 GUE left these shores for Japan in 1982 and is unlikely to return. The survival rate of all the Sabres and Scimitars speaks volumes for the integrity of their construction. One highly modified Sabre 6 (92 FRP) was driven into the record books by the author when it set class records at Prescott and Gurston Down hill climbs in 1984, which remain unbroken three years later.

Joe Devlin racing his well known Sabre 6 at Silverstone.

As owners of later cars joined the club the emphasis of competition has weakened somewhat, certainly on a basis of proportional representation. Also the Coupés and GTEs have displaced the Sabres in many cases as the subject of competition, even though they were never intended for such a role. Even now that some of the cars are over twenty years old, club members are rebuilding and modifying power units and suspensions in an attempt to gain parity with far more modern designs, with amazing results in some cases. Even engine transplants are now being undertaken and possibly the ultimate example of this so far has been Les Trafford's supercharged 4-litre Rover V8 engined hill climb SE5a, with which he won his class in the 1986 Midland Hill Climb Championship.

By 1986 the RSSOC had reached a membership figure in excess of 4,000, which must represent a very high proportion of the Scimitars still registered for road use. Increasing interest in restoration and exhibition of the cars is now evident and this has done far more to improve the respect and value of the older cars in the eyes of enthusiasts than the commendable competition achievements. In that same year the SE5a of Roger Rowley achieved a magnificent result by winning the 'Benson and Hedges' concours outright. By coincidence both Les's hill climb car and Roger's show car are finished in April Yellow and made a very impressive combination at the Brighton Classic Car Show stand in 1986, proving how truly versatile the GTE really was.

The author throwing his faithful SE5a round the Curborough Sprint course in 1977.

The object of many one-make clubs is to offer spares support to its members, but in the RSSOC a number of members have set up businesses purveying spares, so that the general membership is well served by these concerns whose rivalry ensures prices are very competitive. In addition, the experience of long standing members is relayed to newer members by means of a healthy magazine, entitled 'Slice', from which it is possible to build up a picture of the weaknesses and pitfalls in owning and running the various Sabres and Scimitars.

Addresses of Owners Club and Specialists
Reliant Sabre & Scimitar Owners Club; PO Box 67, Northampton NN1 1LR.

Specialists
Attleborough Scimitar Centre, Besthorpe, Attleborough, Norfolk.
Terry Cheshire, Unit 3EG, Waterhall Works, Leeds LS11 5PS.
John Dangerfield Ltd, Staple Hill Road, Fishponds, Bristol.
TC Improvements, Droys Court, Witcombe, Glos GL3 4TN.
Paul Johnson, 48 Ridgewood Avenue, Edenthorpe, Doncaster.
Nigel Newth-Gibbs, 1a Park Lane, Aveley, Essex RM15 4UD.
Queensberry Road Garage, Kettering, Northants.
Robin Rew, Unit 12, Silverstone Circuit, Northants.
Scimpart Ltd., Droys Court, Witcombe, Glos GL3 4TN.
Will Sparrow, Kinwarton Farm Road, Alcester, Warks B49 6EH.
Richard Turnbull, 10 Bradshaw Close, Pogmoor, Barnsley, Yorks.
Graham Walker Ltd., Parkgate Road, Mollington, Chester.

One club specialist, Scimpart Ltd, have modified an accident damaged SE5 to form a very smart and swift pick-up.

WHAT TO LOOK FOR WHEN BUYING SABRES AND SCIMITARS

Sabre 4

Front suspension pivot and king-pin wear, broken springs and worn steering parts, all of which are very rare; rear suspension bushes perished and loose rear axle tubes from suspension strains; rear axle is Reliant built commercial unit for which spares are still available, but ZF gearbox spares virtually unobtainable; Ford engine not too much of a problem, but trim parts inside and out totally obsolete; windscreens re-manufactured but no body panels left; chassis and fuel tank corrosion almost certain on unrestored cars.

Sabre 6

Front suspension bushes wear quickly, but are of TR4 origin and still available; rear axle bushes and axle share problems with the four-cylinder car and parts for the Salisbury 7HA axle are difficult to obtain; chassis outriggers and top or main members prone to corrosion but body easy to remove; engine parts present few problems but overdrive components now obsolete; windscreens and short front bonnets can be obtained but all trim parts and rest of glass unobtainable.

Scimitar GT (SE4)

Front vertical links from Daimler SP250 prone to cracking and now very rare, while rest of chassis and rear axle problems are shared with Sabre 6; gearboxes are either shared with Sabre 4 or 6 with attendant problems; body moulds owned by RSSOC (thanks to Joe Devlin) and complete bodies easily removed from chassis for restoration; windscreens readily available and good supply of used trim and glass can be found from specialists; wire wheels need careful inspection.

Scimitar V6 Coupé (SE4a/b/c)

Later models use TR6 front suspension for which parts are readily available as they are for rear axle but very expensive; narrow rear springs crack in old age; V6 engine and gearbox parts getting scarce, but body, glass and trim parts are similar to SE4 making restoration quite viable; chassis outriggers and lower front suspension anchorages prone to rot but can be repaired in situ.

Scimitar GTE (SE5)

TR6 front suspension is rapid wearing and rear axles need regular maintenance to avoid large bills; chassis outriggers and sills now beginning to need replacement which can be done without removing body; engines are prone to failure of cam timing gear and oil pump drive shaft after high mileages while early gearbox and overdrive parts are now rare; bodywork tends to let in water via gutters and window seals in old age and rear windows and hinges corrode if neglected; front seats reclining mechanism suffers from fatigue; petrol inlet pipe to carburettor can become detached causing fire risk and subject of a recall to pin it in position; most parts still available, new or used; fuel tanks and cooling system pipes corrode; crossflow supergill radiators clog up more easily than in many cars and their efficiency impaired.

Scimitar GTE (SE6/6a)

Suspension, engine, gearbox and axle similar to SE5a, but cooling system different and can give problems if wrong filler cap fitted or cap housing corroded; chassis not showing corrosion yet, but body to chassis bolts can come loose due to greater flexibility of structure; electric window motors have short life and rear windows suffer from loose bracketry; power steering units leak eventually with expensive consequences as do the manual propshafts with constant velocity sealed joints; seats much improved but trim can stain; switchgear can be fragile; early SE6 models suffered from dropping front doors due to structural flexing; all models prone to allowing water into bodywork but unable to retain it in the cooling system, giving rise to an owners' club competition for the largest mushrooms grown in the footwells and rear tool boxes.

Scimitar SE6b/8b

Chassis and running gear identical with SE6 models, but 2.8-litre engine needs same precautions in old age; rear axles apparently less troublesome on these cars and electric window motors improved; electric mirrors and aerials can fail and GTC suffered from water leaks along front rail until Happich catches fitted to later models; engine noisier in GTE/C and naturally more wind noise in GTC; cooling system cured of overheating problem. Body structure now more rigid and chassis galvanised.

Used Model Price Guide

	Date	New Price £	Condition (1987 values £) 3	2	1
Sabre 4	1961	1,164	500	800	2,400
Sabre 6	1963	1,136	600	900	2,500
SE4	1965	1,352	450	900	2,000
SE4a/b	1967	1,577	600	1,000	2,500
SE5	1970	1,825	500	900	2,000
SE5a	1974	2,397	700	1,100	2,800
SE6	1976	4,446	1,200	1,600	3,000
SE6a	1978	6,460	1,500	2,500	4,000
SE6b	1980	11,790	3,500	5,000	7,000
SE8b	1980	12,490	4,500	7,000	10,000

Appendix

	page
Summary of four-wheeled Reliants	202
GTE family tree	203
Chassis numbers	204
Chassis number codes	205
Sabre 4 specification	206
Sabre 6 specification	208
SE4 specification	210
SE4a/b specification	212
SE5/5a specification	214
SE6/6a specification	216
SE6b specification	218
SE8b specification	220
SS1 specification	222
Performance table	224
Wheel options	225

SUMMARY OF RELIANT 4-WHEELED MODELS

ECONOMY RANGE

FW1	—	REGENT IV Van for Israel (SUSSITA MkI)
FW2	—	REGENT Van MkII for Israel (SUSSITA MkII)
FW3	—	CARMEL car, van and estate for Israel
FW4	—	REBEL 750 car and estate
FW5	—	ANADOL for Turkey
FW6	—	REBEL 1600GT — no production
FW7	—	Mid-Engined 850cc Ogle-bodied two seater — prototype only
FW8	—	Replacement BOND EQUIPÉ — no production
FW9	—	four-wheeled TW9 ANT commercial — no production
FW10	—	KITTEN saloon and estate
FW10a	—	FOX pick-up
FW11	—	Bertone-bodied ANADOL replacement — no production

SPORTS CAR RANGE

SE1	—	SABRE 4 two seater sports and Coupé (208 produced)
SE2	—	SABRE 6 GT Coupé (77 produced)
SE3	—	V8-engined GT car — abandoned
SE4	—	Straight-Six SCIMITAR Coupé (297 produced)
SE4a/b	—	3-litre V6 SCIMITAR Coupé (591 produced)
SE4c	—	2.5-litre V6 SCIMITAR Coupé (118 produced)
SE5	—	SCIMITAR GTE 3-litre (4,311 produced)
SE5a	—	Uprated SE5 (5,105 produced)
SE6	—	Enlarged GTE 3-litre (543 produced)
SE6a	—	Improved SE6 (3877 produced)
SE6b	—	2.8-litre SE6 GTE (437 produced)
SE7	—	four door version of the SE6 — abandoned
SE8b	—	2.8-litre GTC convertible (442 produced)
SE82	—	Bertone-bodied V8 GTE replacement — prototype only
SS1	—	Michelotti-designed two seater 1,300cc and 1,600cc — in production
1800ti	—	Nissan Turbo-engined version of SS1 — in production

APPENDIX   *203*

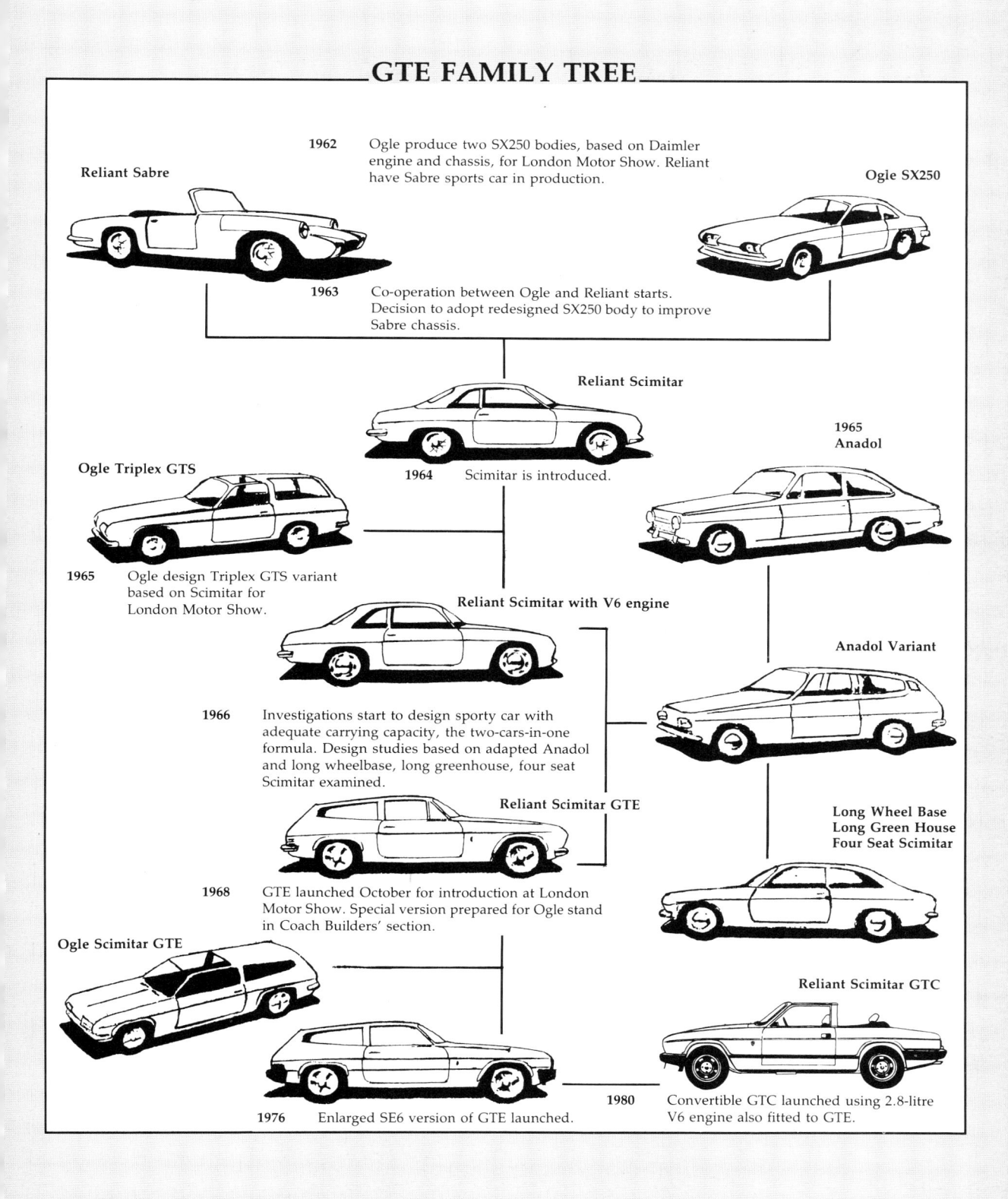

GTE FAMILY TREE

Reliant Sabre

1962 Ogle produce two SX250 bodies, based on Daimler engine and chassis, for London Motor Show. Reliant have Sabre sports car in production.

Ogle SX250

1963 Co-operation between Ogle and Reliant starts. Decision to adopt redesigned SX250 body to improve Sabre chassis.

Reliant Scimitar

1964 Scimitar is introduced.

1965 Anadol

Ogle Triplex GTS

1965 Ogle design Triplex GTS variant based on Scimitar for London Motor Show.

Reliant Scimitar with V6 engine

Anadol Variant

1966 Investigations start to design sporty car with adequate carrying capacity, the two-cars-in-one formula. Design studies based on adapted Anadol and long wheelbase, long greenhouse, four seat Scimitar examined.

Reliant Scimitar GTE

Long Wheel Base Long Green House Four Seat Scimitar

1968 GTE launched October for introduction at London Motor Show. Special version prepared for Ogle stand in Coach Builders' section.

Ogle Scimitar GTE

Reliant Scimitar GTC

1976 Enlarged SE6 version of GTE launched.

1980 Convertible GTC launched using 2.8-litre V6 engine also fitted to GTE.

SABRE & SCIMITAR CHASSIS RECORDS

Model	Year	Start	Finish	Comments
Sabre 4	1961 (Mar)	S200001	S200097	Open sports 4 cyl developed from SABRA
(SE1)	1962	S200098	S200174	FH Coupé announced in June (S200130)
	1963	S200175	S200208	Bonnet shortened in June (S200201)
Sabre 6	1962 (Oct)	SS300001	SS300004	FH Coupé only, S/Six engine
(SE2)	1963	SS300005	SS300146	SS300005 & 300120 open sports
	1964	SS300147	SS300177	Final chassis only one to be exported
Scimitar GT	1965	SC400001	SC400119	Rear suspension changed SC400059
(SE4)	1966	SC400120	SC400297	S/Six production ceased in October
(SE4a)	1966 (Oct)	SC400401	SC400424	2,994cc V6 engine introduced
	1967	SC400425	SC400635	
	1968	SC400636	SC400939	SE4b introduced SC400901 with internal modifications and vented disc wheels
(SE4b)	1969	SC400940	SC400973	
	1970	SC400974	SC400991	Production ceased in November
(SE4c)	1967 (Aug)	SC425001	SC425049	2.5-litre V6 version of Coupé
	1968	SC425050	SC425104	
	1969	SC425105	SC425114	
	1970	SC425115	SC425118	Production ceased in November 1970
Scimitar GTE	1968 (Aug)	450001	450101	3-litre Man/Overdrive Sports Estate
(SE5)	1969	450102	450740	
	1970	450741	451734	Automatic introduced 451729
	1971	451735	451821	
	1972	452822	454311	Uprated Granada engine from 453501
(SE5a)	1972 (Oct)	93x1001	93x1601	Revised interior, grille & rear lights
	1973	93x1602	93x3721	
	1974	93x3722	93x5909	511 chassis nos. not used
	1975	93x5910	93x6615	Production ceased October
(SE6)	1975	5M4918301008	5M4718301015	Larger body and revised interior
	1976	6A4418101016	6H4818101550	
(SE6a)	1976	6H4818101552	6M4018302231	Structural mods. & Lockheed brakes
	1977	7A4318302232	7M4718103804	
	1978	8A4418103805	8M5818404648	
	1979	9A5818404649	1840559L005428	International chassis code introduced
(SE6b)	1979	1903559L005429	1903609M005493	2.8-litre V6 introduced, lower axle ratio
	1980	190155AF005494	190160AM005568	
	1981	190311BA005569	190362BM005609	
	1982	190158CA005610	190199CM005674	
	1983	190199DA005675	190199DM005753	
	1984	190399EA005754	190176EM005836	
	1985	190199FA005837	190156FL005857	
	1986	190155GA005858	190199GD005865	
Scimitar GTC	1980	20035AA000001	200162AL000340	Convertible version with 2.8-litre engine
(SE8b)	1981	200166BB000341	200165BJ000343	
	1982	200362CA000344	200199CM000363	
	1983	200155DA000364	200399DM000387	
	1984	200399EA000388	200399EM000416	
	1985	200155FA000417	200376FL000429	
	1986	200368GA000430	200135GC000442	Production ceased in November
SS1 1300	1984	210171EL000007	210170EM000027	Brand new two seater 4 cyl sports
	1985	210170FA000028	210170FM000719	
	1986	210183GA000738	210171GM000996	Galvanised chassis introduced at 900
SS1 1600	1984	210270EL000003	210270EL000009	Ford XR3 carburettor engine
	1985	210271FA000037	210282FM000732	
	1986	210271GA000733	210272GM000995	Galvanised chassis introduced from 900
1800Ti	1986	210574GF000841	210599GM000994	Nissan Turbo 1,800cc fuel inj. engine

APPENDIX

CHASSIS NUMBER CODING

With the introduction of the SE6 in October 1975, Reliant employed a new system of chassis numbering intended to give more information to both Dealers and the Reliant Motor Co. in the future. The composition of these numbers is as follows, using the first chassis number as an example:

$$5\ J\ 48\ 182\ 01001$$

Year
Last figure only
e.g. 1975 is 5

Month
Jan = A
Feb = B
etc.
I not used so
Sept = J

Paint Colour
See list below

Model
181 — Overdrive Man. steer
182 — Overdrive Power steer
183 — Automatic Man. steer
184 — Automatic Power steer

Serial No.
Starting with 01001

In 1979 International regulations were introduced whereby every car manufacturer had to identify each car produced with a 17-digit chassis number including the manufacturer's Identity code, date of production and colour at least. Thus Reliant had to comply during the production run of the SE6a when the composition of the chassis numbers was altered as follows using the first such number issued as an example:

$$SCD\ 19\ 03\ 55\ 9\ L\ 005429$$

Manufacturer
Identity Code
i.e. Reliant

Vehicle Code
19 — GTE
20 — GTC
21 — SS1
22 — SST

Model Code
01 — Overdrive
03 — Automatic
01 — SS1 1300
02 — SS1 1600
05 — 1800 Ti

Paint Code
See list below

Year
Last figure only
i.e. 1979 is 9.
After 1980
letters used
i.e. 1980 is A

Month
Jan = A
Feb = B
I not used
so Sept — J

Serial No.
consec.

Paint Codes

11 — Olympic Blue	43 — Arctic/Everest White	60 — Buckskin
12 — Festival Red	44 — April Yellow No. 2	61 — Aztec Blue
13 — Parrot Green	45 — Beaujolais Red	62 — White Rose
14 — Riviera Brown	46 — Ivory Beige	63 — Lincoln Green
15 — Yellow Ochre	47 — Sierra Tan	64 — Russet Red
16 — Sierra Tan	48 — Lincoln Green	65 — Celtic Brown
18 — Mexico Brown	49 — Caspian Blue	66 — Aquamarine
19 — Capricorn Blue	50 — Dolphin Grey	67 — Stunning Red
20 — Mineral Blue	51 — Greengage Yellow	68 — Panama
21 — Florida Green	52 — Russet Red	70 — Frost White
22 — Tangerine	53 — Quartz Green	71 — Scimitar Red
23 — Sahara Red	54 — Mulberry	72 — Racing Green
31 — Bajan Blue	55 — Carmen	73 — Derwent Blue
32 — Haze Blue	56 — Champagne	74 — Birch Silver
33 — Willow Green	57 — Silver Birch	81 — Brecon Gold
41 — Cygnet Grey	58 — Trafalgar Blue	82 — Tarn Green
42 — Alaska Blue	59 — Eldorado	83 — Istrian Blue

} SS1 colours

RELIANT SABRE 4

ENGINE
- Cylinders .. .. 4 in line
- Bore 82.6mm (3.25in)
- Stroke 79.5mm (3.13in)
- Displacement .. 1,703cc (103.9cu in)
- Valve gear .. Overhead, pushrods and rockers
- Compression ratio .. 8.8 to 1
- Carburettor .. Single Zenith 34VN downdraught
- Fuel Pump .. AC mechanical
- Oil filter .. .. Full-flow external, replaceable element
- Max power (net) .. 71.5bhp at 4,400rpm
- Max torque .. 91lb ft at 2,300rpm

TRANSMISSION
- Clutch .. .. 8.5in single dry plate
- Gearbox .. .. ZF four-speed, all-synchromesh
- Overall ratios .. Top 3.55; Third 4.37; Second 6.00; First 9.00
- Final drive .. Spiral bevel, 3.55 to 1
- Chassis .. .. Separate steel frame with parallel boxed side members
- Body .. .. Moulded glass fibre

SUSPENSION
- Front .. .. Independent, with single leading arms giving semi-swing-axle geometry, Girling coil spring and co-axial telescopic damper units
- Rear .. .. Live axle located by modified Watts linkage, Girling coil spring and co-axial damper units
- Steering .. Reliant rack and pinion. Three-spoke light alloy Carlotti wheel with wooden rim, 15in dia

BRAKES
- Type .. .. Girling hydraulic; discs front, drums rear, no servo
- Dimensions .. F, 10.5in discs, R, 9in drums, 1.75in wide shoes
- Swept areas .. F, 202sq in; R, 99sq in. Total 301sq in (312sq in per ton laden)

WHEELS
- Type .. .. Standard: Pierced steel disc, 4 studs, 4.25in wide rims. Extra: wire-spoked with centre-lock hubs, 4.25in wide rims
- Tyres .. .. 155-15 Pirelli Cintura with tubes

EQUIPMENT
- Battery .. .. 12-volt, 38amp hr
- Headlamps .. Lucas sealed beam, 60-45 watt filaments
- Reversing lamp .. None
- Electric fuses .. 2
- Screen wipers .. Two blades, single-speed, self-parking
- Screen washers .. Electrical pump type
- Interior heater .. Fresh air heater-demister with single-speed fan standard
- Safety belts .. Anchorages provided
- Interior trim .. Leathercloth on standard seats. Aero-style seats, with woven fabric and pvc trim, extra
- Floor covering .. Pile carpeting
- Starting handle .. None
- Jack .. .. Screw pillar with ratchet handle
- Jacking points .. Front, under bonnet, welded to suspension arms; rear, under body sills, forward of rear wheel arches
- Other bodies .. Detachable hardtop

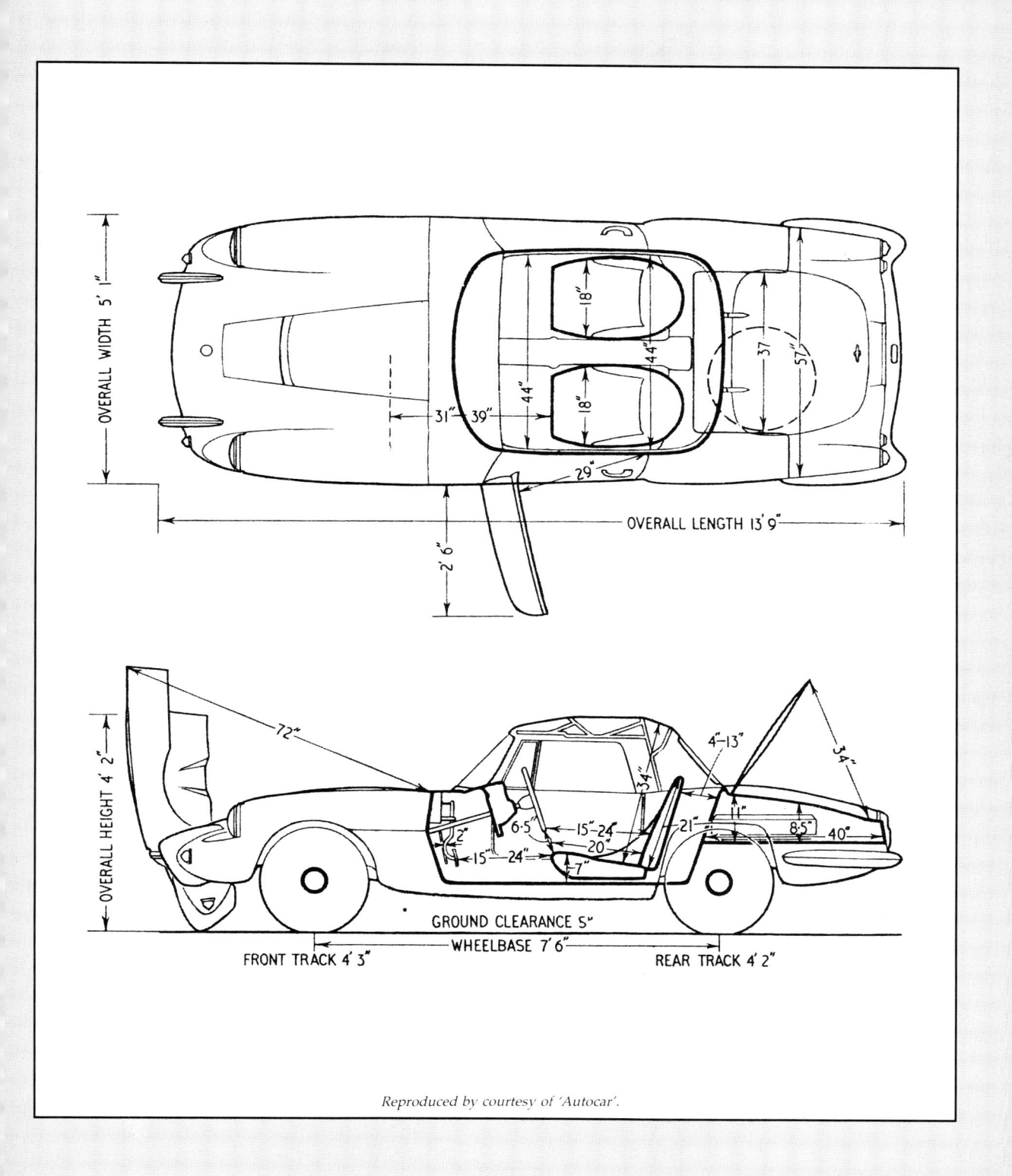

Appendix

Reproduced by courtesy of 'Autocar'.

RELIANT SABRE SIX GT

PERFORMANCE DATA
Overdrive top gear mph per 1,000rpm 26.1
Top gear mph per 1,000rpm 20.1
Mean piston speed at max. power 2,490ft/min
Engine revs at mean max speed 4,180rpm
Bhp per ton laden 87.2

ENGINE
Cylinders 6-in-line
Bore 82.6mm (3.25in)
Stroke 79.5mm (3.13in)
Displacement .. 2,553cc (159cu in)
Valve gear .. Overhead, pushrods and rockers
Compression ratio 8.3-to-1
Carburettor .. Zenith
Fuel Pump .. AC mechanical
Oil filter .. .. Full-flow, renewable element
Max power .. 109bhp (net) at 4,800rpm
 137lb ft at 2,400rpm

TRANSMISSION
Clutch .. .. Single dry-plate, 8.8in dia.
Gearbox .. .. Four-speed all synchromesh
Ratios .. .. OD Top 0.77; Top 1.0;
 OD Third 1.19; Third 1.41;
 OD Second 1.70; Second 2.21;
 OD First 2.43; First 3.16;
 Reverse 3.34
Final drive .. Hypoid, 3.58 to 1

CHASSIS
Construction .. Box section chassis, with glass fibre bodywork

SUSPENSION
Front .. .. Independent, coil springs, wishbones, telescopic dampers
Rear .. .. Live axle, coil springs, modified Watts linkage, telescopic dampers
Steering .. .. Rack and pinion
Wheel dia .. 15in

BRAKES
Type .. .. Girling hydraulic, disc front, drum rear
Dimensions .. F, 10.4in dia, R, 9in dia; 1.57in wide shoes
Swept area .. F, 110sq in; R, 99sq in. Total: 209sq in (198sq in per ton laden)

WHEELS
Type .. .. Pressed-steel disc standard; wire spoke, centre lock extra 4.5in wide rim
Tyres .. .. 165 — 15in Pirelli Cinturato with tubes

EQUIPMENT
Battery .. .. 12-volt 57amp hr
Headlamps .. Lucas sealed beam
Reversing lamp .. None
Electric fuses .. None
Screen wipers .. 2, two-speed
Screenwasher .. Standard, vacuum operated
Interior heater .. Standard, fresh air
Safety belts .. Extra, anchorages not provided
Interior trim .. Pvc
Floor covering .. Carpet
Starting handle .. No provision
Jack .. .. Scissors Type
Jacking points .. Under chassis
Other bodies .. Open sports

MAINTENANCE
Fuel tank .. .. 12 Imp gallons (no reserve)
Cooling system .. 23 pints (inc heater)
Engine sump .. 8.5 pints SAE20. Change oil every 5,000 miles; change filter element every 5,000 miles
Gearbox and over-
drive .. .. 5 pints SAE80EP. Change oil every 10,000 miles
Final drive .. 2 pints SAE90. Change oil every 10,000 miles
Grease .. .. 18 points every 1,000 miles
Tyre pressures .. F and R, 26psi (normal driving)
 F and R, 29psi (fast driving)

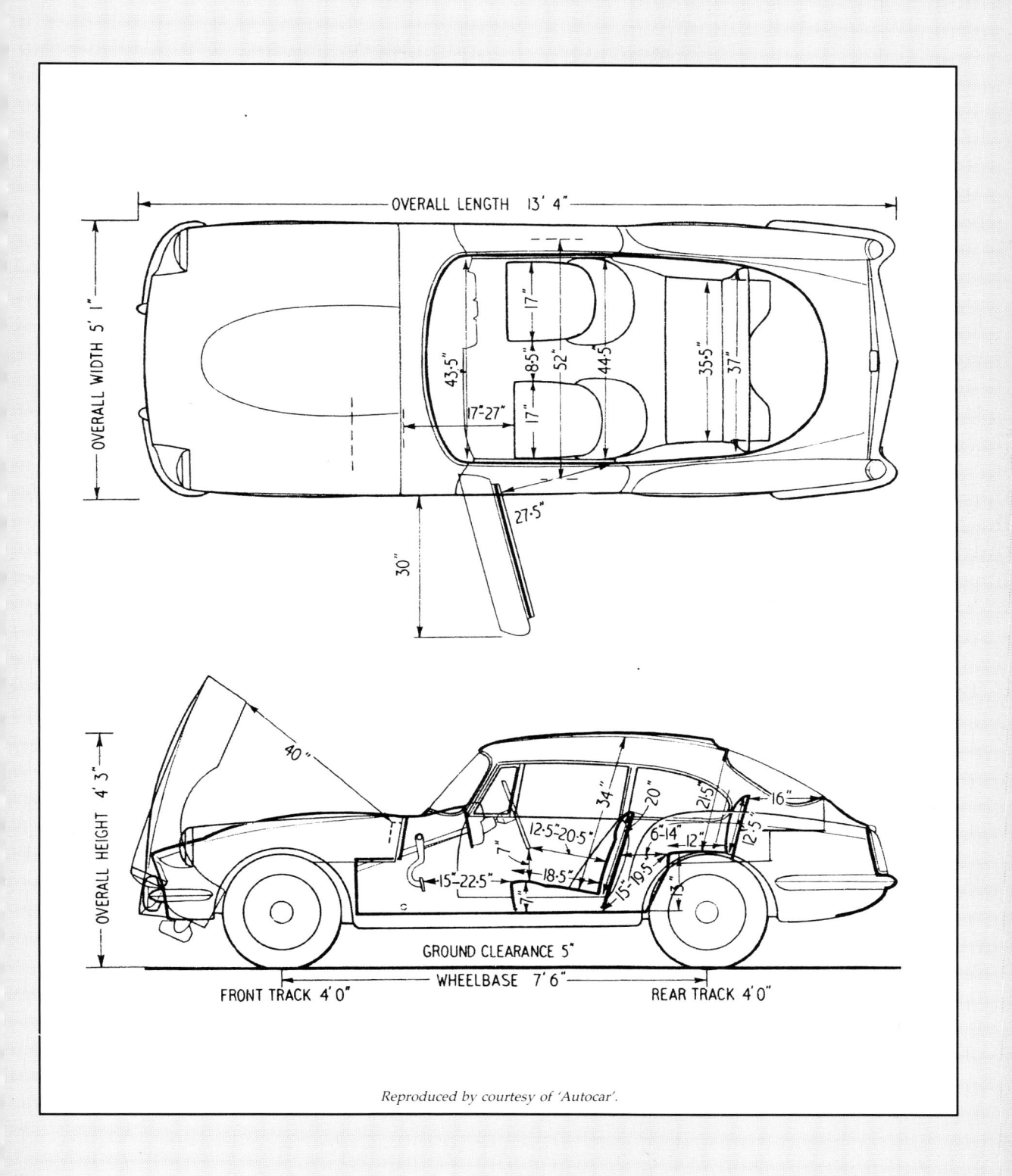

Appendix

Reproduced by courtesy of 'Autocar'.

RELIANT SCIMITAR GT SE4

ENGINE
Cylinders 6-in-line
Cooling system .. Water; pump, fan and thermostat
Bore 82.55mm (3.25in)
Stroke 79.50mm (3.13in)
Displacement .. 2,553cc (155.8cu in)
Valve gear .. Overhead, pushrods and rockers
Compression ratio 8.3-to-1
Carburettors .. 3 S.U. type HS4
Fuel pump .. A.C. mechanical
Oil filter .. .. A.C. full-flow, renewable element
Max power .. 120bhp (net) at 5,000rpm
Max torque .. 140lb ft (net) at 2,600rpm

TRANSMISSION
Clutch .. .. Single dry plate, 8.5in dia.
Gearbox .. .. 4-speed, all-synchromesh
Gear ratios .. OD Top 0.778; Top 1.0; OD Third 1.10; Third 1.4; Second 2.21; First 3.16; Reverse 3.35
Final drive .. Spiral bevel, 3.88-to-1

CHASSIS and BODY
Construction .. Pressed steel box-section frame with separate glass fibre body

SUSPENSION
Front .. .. Independent, wishbones and coil springs, telescopic dampers
Rear .. .. Live axle, coil springs, modified Watts linkage, telescopic dampers
Steering .. .. Rack and pinion
Wheel dia 15.25in

BRAKES
Make and Type .. Girling disc front, drum rear
Servo .. .. Girling Powerstop, vacuum type
Dimensions .. F, 10.6in dia; R, 9in dia; 1.75in wide shoes
Swept area .. F, 227sq in; R, .99sq in. Total 326sq in (264sq in per ton laden)

WHEELS
Type .. .. Centre-lock, wire spokes
Tyres .. .. Pirelli Cinturato tubed
Size .. .. 165 — 15in

EQUIPMENT
Battery .. .. 12-volt 57amp hr
Generator .. Lucas
Headlamps .. Lucas sealed beam, 55-37.5 watt
Reversing lamp .. Extra
Electric fuses .. 2
Screen wipers .. 2-speed, self-parking
Screen washer .. Standard, vacuum-type
Interior heater .. Standard, fresh-air type
Safety belts .. Extra, anchorages provided
Interior trim .. Cloth and pvc seats, pvc headlining
Floor covering .. Carpet
Starting handle .. No provision
Jack .. .. Scissors type
Jacking points .. Under chassis
Other bodies .. None

MAINTENANCE
Fuel tank .. .. 20 Imp gallons (no reserve) (91 litres)
Cooling system .. 23 pints (including heater) (13 litres)
Engine sump .. 6.5 pints (3.7 litres) SAE 20/30. Change oil every 5,000 miles. Change filter element every 5,000 miles
Gearbox and over drive .. 5 pints SAE 80EP. Change oil every 5,000 miles
Final drive .. 2 pints SAE90. Change oil every 5,000 miles
Grease .. .. 15 points every 5,000 miles
Tyre pressures .. F, 26; R, 26psi (normal driving). F, 26; R, 28psi (full load)

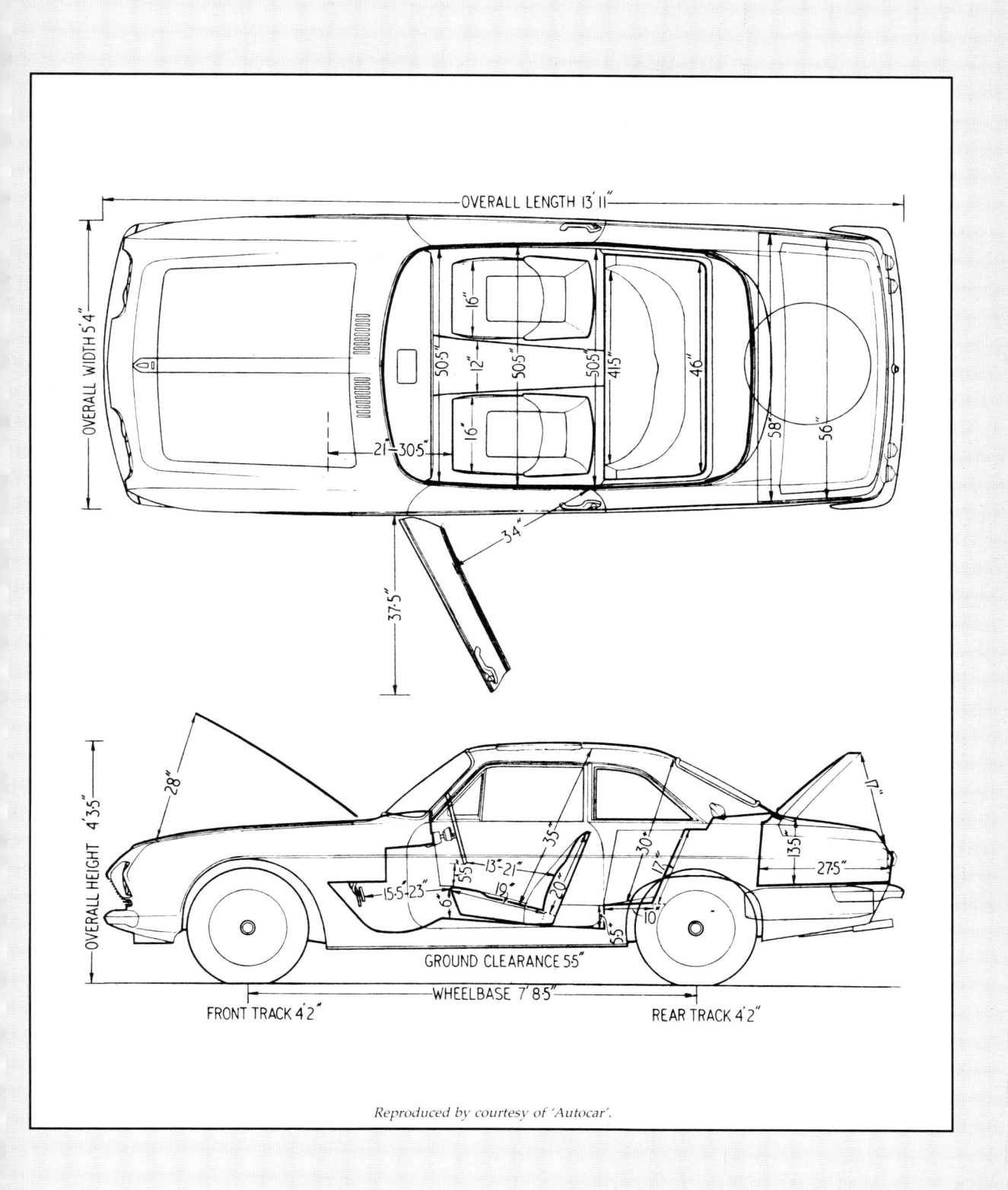

Appendix

RELIANT SCIMITAR COUPÉ SE4a

PERFORMANCE DATA
Top gear mph per 1,000rpm 20.2
Overdrive top mph per 1,000rpm 24.6
Mean piston speed at max. power 2,260ft/min
Bhp per ton laden 106.5

ENGINE
Cylinders	6, in 60-deg. vee
Cooling system	Water; pump, fan and thermostat
Bore	93.7mm (3.69in)
Stroke	72.4mm (2.85in)
Displacement	2,994cc (182.7cu in)
Valve gear	Overhead, pushrods and rockers
Compression ratio	8.9-to-1
Carburettor	Weber twin choke 40 DFA-1
Fuel Pump	AC mechanical
Oil filter	Full-flow, renewable element
Max power	136bhp (net) at 4,750rpm
Max torque	192lb ft at 3,000rpm

TRANSMISSION
Clutch	Single dry plate, 9in dia, diaphragm spring
Gearbox	4-speed, all-synchromesh with overdrive on third and top
Gear ratios	OD Top 0.82; Top 1.0; OD Third 1.16; Third 1.41; Second 2.21; First 3.16 Reverse 3.33
Final drive	Hypoid bevel, 3.58 to 1

CHASSIS and BODY
Construction	Pressed steel box-section frame with separate glass fibre body

SUSPENSION
Front	Independent, wishbones and coil springs, telescopic dampers, anti-roll bar
Rear	Live axle, coil springs, trailing arms, modified Watts linkage, telescopic dampers

STEERING
Type	Rack and pinion Wheel dia 15in

BRAKES
Make and Type	Girling disc front, drum rear
Servo	Girling Powerstop, vacuum type
Dimensions	F, 10.63in dia; R, 9in dia. 1.75in wide shoes
Swept area	F, 227sq in; R, 99sq in. Total 326sq in (256sq in per ton laden)

WHEELS
Type	Pressed-steel disc, 4-stud fixing, 5.5in wide rim
Tyres — make	Pirelli
— type	Cinturato tubed radial-ply
— size	165 — 15in

EQUIPMENT
Battery	12-volt 57amp hr
Alternator	Lucas type 11AC 35 amp
Headlamps	4 Lucas sealed beam 37.5/50-watt
Reversing lamp	2
Electric fuses	2
Screen wipers	2-speed, self-parking
Screen washer	Standard, vacuum-type
Interior heater	Standard, water valve control
Safety belts	Extra
Interior trim	Leathercloth seats, pvc headlining
Floor covering	Carpet
Starting handle	No provision
Jack	Scissors Type
Jacking points	Under chassis
Windscreen	Zone toughened (laminated option fitted)
Underbody protection	Non-corrosive glassfibre body; painted steel chassis
Other bodies	None

MAINTENANCE
Fuel tank	21.3 Imp gallons (no reserve) (96 litres)
Cooling system	22 pints (including heater) (12.5 litres)
Engine sump	9.5 pints (5.4 litres) SAE 10W/30. Change oil every 10,000 miles. Change filter element every 10,000 miles
Gearbox and overdrive	4.25 pints SAE 80. Change oil every 10,000 miles
Final drive	2.0 pints SAE 90EP. Change oil every 10,000 miles
Grease	15 points every 5,000 miles
Tyre pressures	F, 26; R, 26psi (normal driving). F, 28; R, 28psi (fast driving)

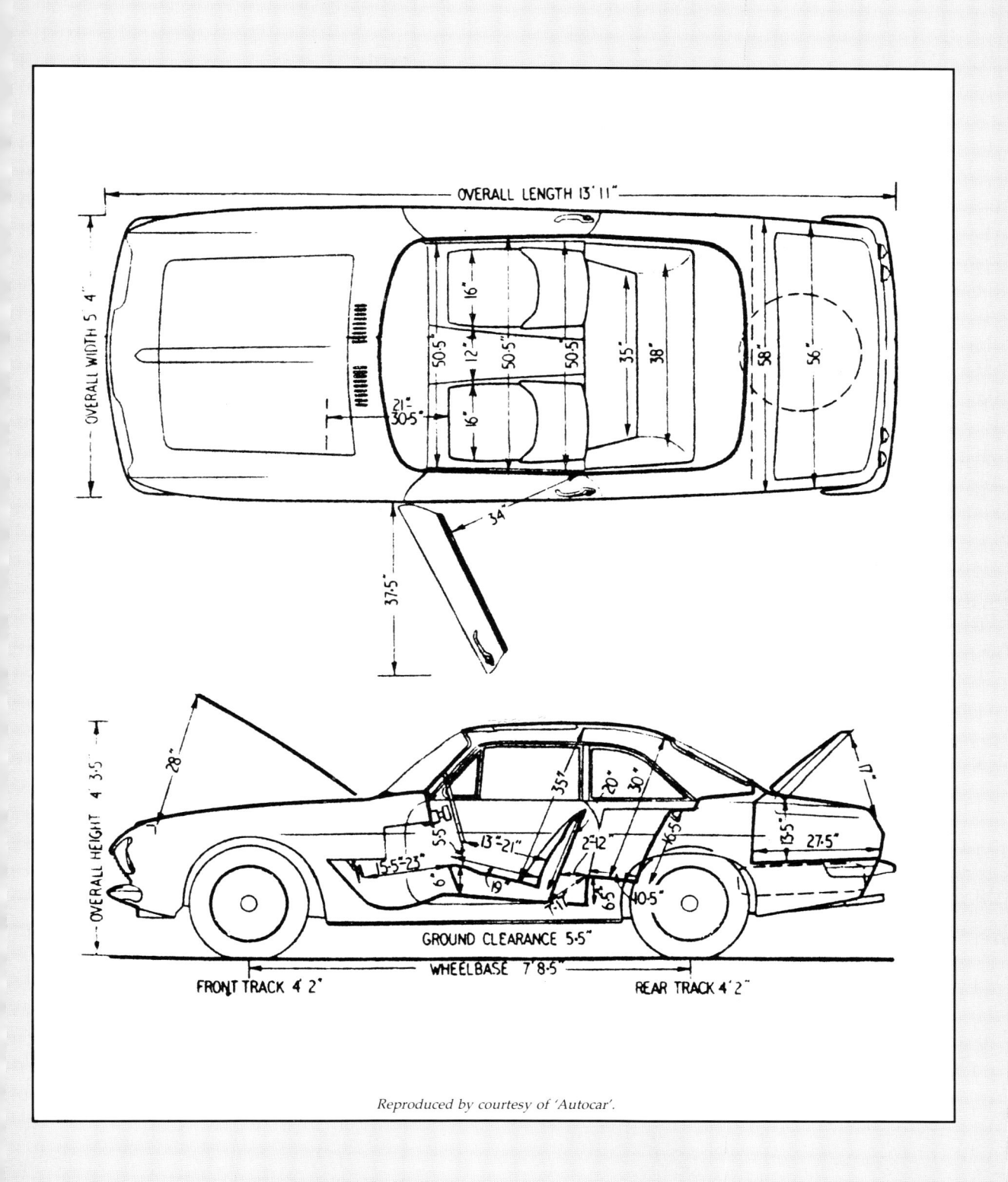

APPENDIX

Reproduced by courtesy of 'Autocar'.

RELIANT SCIMITAR SE5/5a

ENGINE
Block material	Cast iron
Head material	Cast iron
Cylinders	60 deg V-6
Cooling system	Water, pressurised system
Bore and stroke	93.67mm (3.69in) 72.42mm (2.85in)
Cubic capacity	2,994cc (182.7cu in)
Main bearings	3
Valves	Ohv pushrod
Compression ratio	8.9:1
Carburettor	Weber 40 DFA-1
Fuel pump	AC Delco mechanical
Oil filter	AC Delco full flow
Max power (din)	138bhp at 5,000rpm
Max torque (din)	172lb ft at 3,000rpm

TRANSMISSION
Clutch .. Borg and Beck sdp 9in diameter

Internal gearbox ratios:

	Manual	O/drive	Auto
Top gear	1.00:1	1.00:1	—
3rd gear	1.41:1	1.41:1	1.00:1
2nd gear	1.95:1	1.95:1	1.47:1
1st gear	3.16:1	3.16:1	2.47:1
Reverse	3.35:1	3.35:1	2.11:1
Overdrive top	—	0.78:1	—
Final drive	3.07:1	3.31:1	3.07:1
Top gear mph/ 1,000 rpm	23.5	28.4	23.5

CHASSIS AND BODY
Construction .. Steel box frame chassis with side members supporting glass-fibre body

BRAKES
Type	Girling hydraulic, disc/drum
Dimensions	10.63in disc, 9 × 1.75in drums

Friction areas:
- Front: 24sq in of lining operating on 227sq in of disc
- Rear: 88.5sq in of lining operating on 99sq in of drum

SUSPENSION AND STEERING
Front	Independent by coil springs and wishbones
Rear	Live axle located by parallel trailing arms and Watt linkage; coil spring/damper units

Shock absorbers:
- Front: Telescopic
- Rear: Telescopic

Steering type	Rack and pinion, Cam Gear
Tyres	185 × 14 Cinturato SR
Wheels	14in
Rim size	5½J
Tyre pressures	24psi F&R

COACHWORK AND EQUIPMENT
Starting handle	No
Tool kit contents	Jack, jack handle, wheel brace
Jack	Scissor screw
Jacking points	Under chassis frame
Battery	12 volt negative earth 57 amp hrs capacity
Number of electrical fuses	8
Indicators	Self cancelling flashers
Reversing lamp	Yes
Screen wipers	Two speed electric
Screen washers	Electric, push button
Sun visors	2

Locks:
- With ignition key: doors
- With other keys: tailgate

Interior heater	Fresh air unit fitted as standard
Upholstery	Pvc
Floor covering	Carpet
Alternative body styles	Scimitar 2 + 2
Maximum load	900lb
Major extras available	Overdrive

MAINTENANCE
Fuel tank capacity	17 galls
Sump	9.5 pints SAE 10W30
Gearbox	3.25 pints SAE 80
Rear axle	2 pints SAE 90 E.P.
Steering gear	Castrolease LM
Coolant	23 pints (2 drain taps)
Chassis lubrication	Every 3,000 miles to 5 points
Minimum service interval	3,000 miles
Ignition timing	12deg btdc
Contact breaker gap	0.015in
Sparking plug gap	0.025in
Sparking plug type	Autolite A622
Tappet clearances (cold)	Inlet 0.012in; Exhaust 0.020in

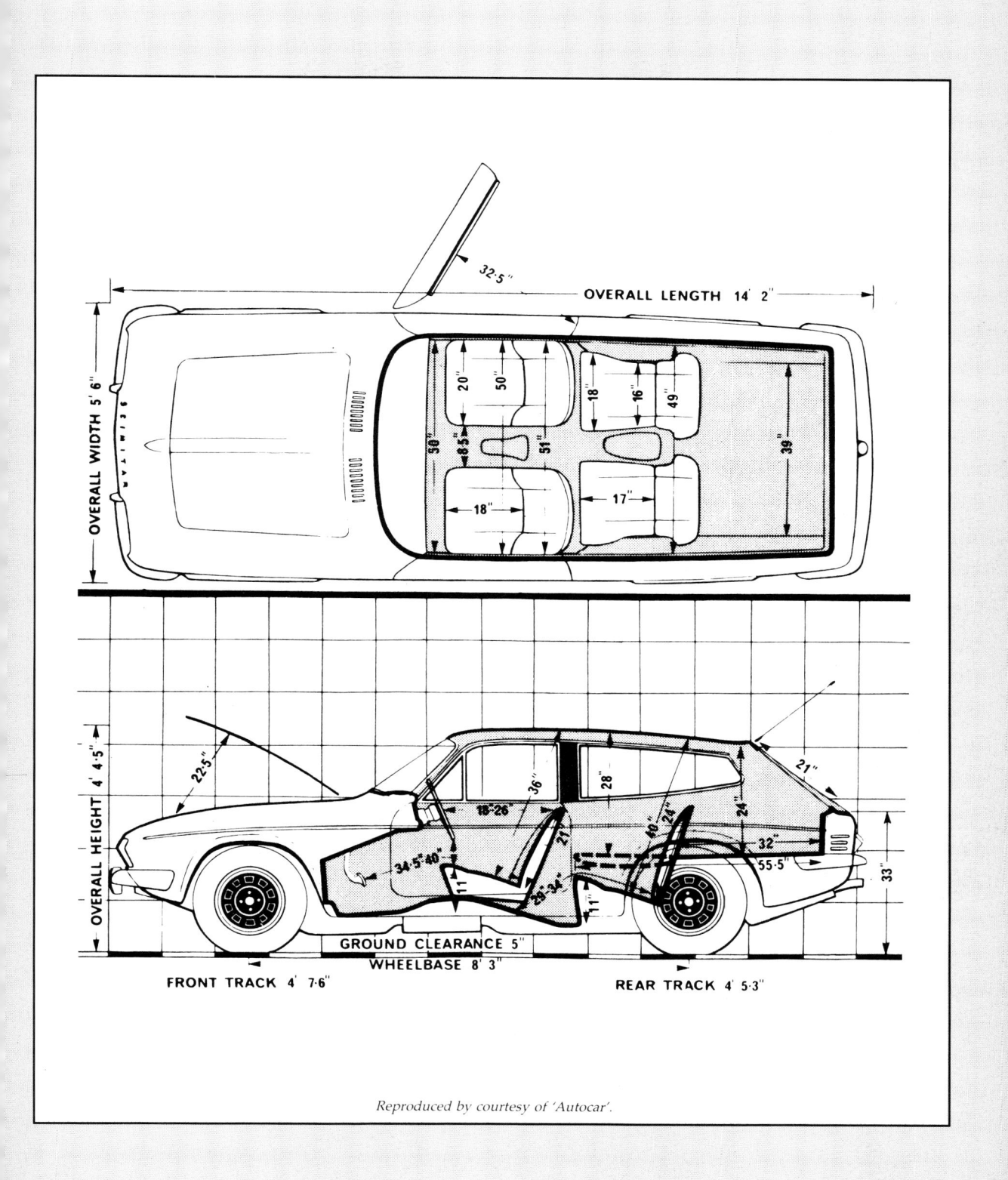

APPENDIX

Reproduced by courtesy of 'Autocar'.

RELIANT SCIMITAR SE6/6a

ENGINE Front, rear drive
Cylinders .. .. Six in 60 degs vee
Main bearings .. 4
Cooling .. .. Water
Fan .. .. Electric
Bore 93.67mm (3.69in)
Stroke 72.42mm (2.85in)
Capacity .. .. 2,994cc (182.7cu in)
Valve gear .. Ohv
Camshaft drive .. Fibre gears
Compression ratio 8.9-to-1
Octane rating .. 97 RM
Carburettor .. Weber 38 DGAS/3A
Max power .. 135bhp (DIN) at 5,500rpm
Max torque .. 172lb ft at 3,000rpm

TRANSMISSION
Type   Four-speed manual with overdrive

Gear	Ratio	mph/1,000rpm
Top o/d	0.778	28.36
Top	1.000	22.07
3rd o/d	1.098	20.10
3rd	1.412	15.63
2nd	1.950	11.32
1st	3.163	6.98

Final drive gear .. Hypoid bevel
Ratio 3.31-to-1

SUSPENSION
Front — location .. Wishbones
  — springs .. Coil
  — dampers .. Telescopic
  — anti-roll bar .. Yes
Rear — location   Live axle, parallel trailing arms, Watts linkage
  — springs .. Coil
  — dampers .. Telescopic
  — anti-roll bar .. No

STEERING
Type .. .. Rack and pinion
Power assistance .. Option
Wheel diameter .. 14.8in

BRAKES
Front .. .. 10.5in dia disc
Rear .. .. 10.0in dia drum
Servo .. .. Yes

WHEELS
Type .. .. Pressed steel disc
Rim width .. 5½inJ
Tyres — make .. Dunlop
  — type .. Radial tubeless
  — size .. 185HR 14

EQUIPMENT
Battery 12v 55Ah
Alternator .. .. 36 amp
Headlamps .. 60/45-watt outer, 50-watt inner
Reversing lamp .. Standard
Hazard warning .. Standard
Electric fuses .. 12
Screen wipers .. Two-speed
Screen washer .. Electric
Interior heater .. Air blending
Interior trim .. Cloth seats, cloth headlining
Floor covering .. Carpet
Jack .. .. Scissor
Jacking points .. Four, under chassis
Windscreen .. Toughened
Underbody
  protection .. Submerged dip for chassis, GRP body

MAINTENANCE
Fuel tank .. .. 20 Imp gal (91 litres)
Cooling system .. 17 pints (inc heater)
Engine sump .. 8.8 pints SAE 20W/50
Gearbox .. .. 5 pints SAE 80 E.P.
Final drive .. 2 pints SAE 90 E.P.
Grease .. .. 4 points
Valve clearance .. Inlet .031in (hot), Exhaust .020in (hot)
Contact breaker .. 0.025in gap
Ignition timing .. 14deg BTDC (static)
Spark plug
  — type .. Motorcraft AGR 22
  — gap .. 0.025in
Tyre pressures .. F 24; R 24psi (normal driving)
Max payload .. 930lb 423kg

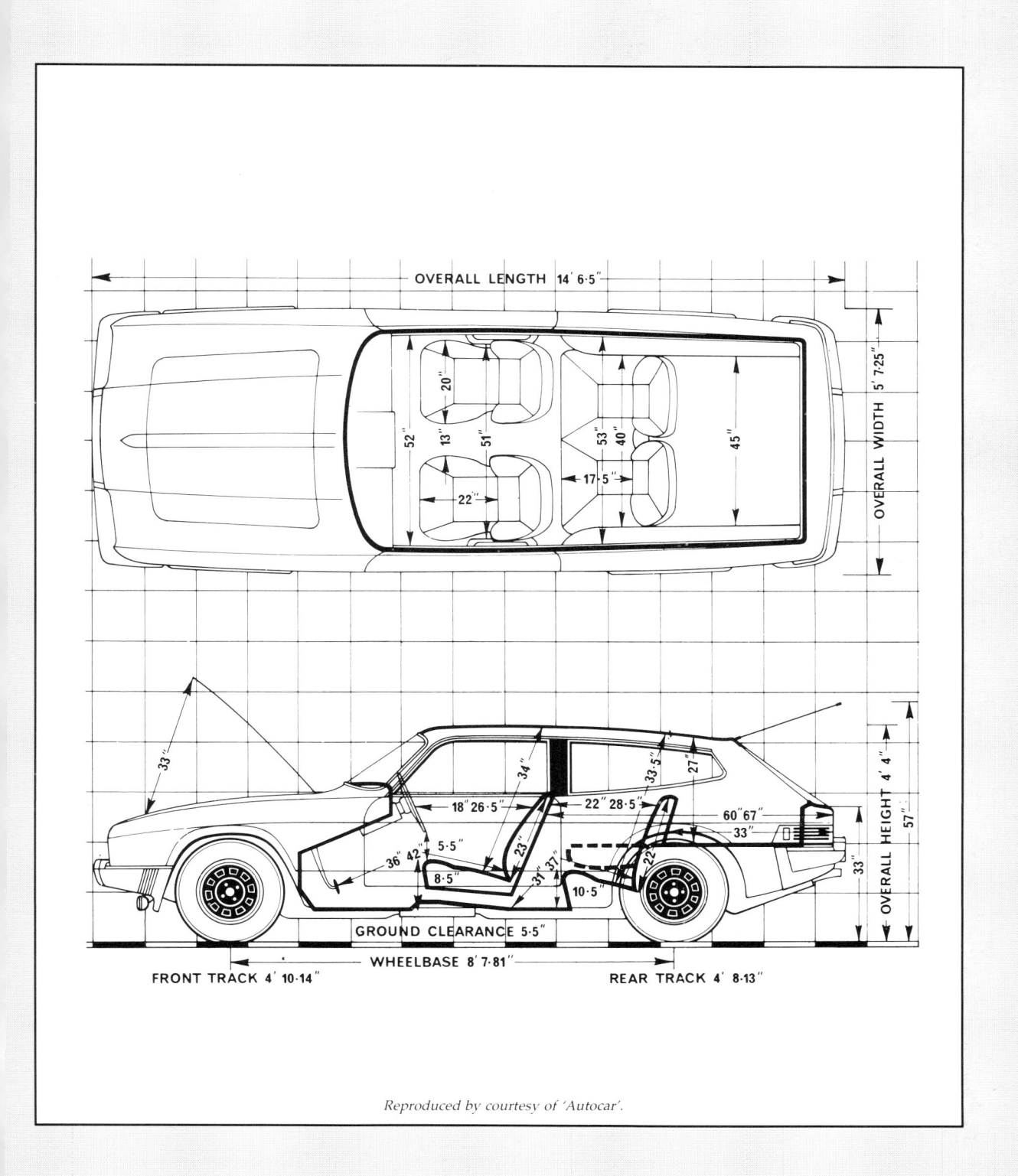

APPENDIX

Reproduced by courtesy of 'Autocar'.

RELIANT SCIMITAR SE6b

ENGINE
Head block	Cast iron
Cylinders	6, in 60deg vee
Main bearing	4
Cooling	Water
Fan	Electric
Bore	93.02mm (3.66in)
Stroke	68.50mm (2.70in)
Capacity	2,792cc (170.38cu in)
Valve gear	Ohv
Camshaft drive	gears
Compression ratio	9.2-to-1
Ignition	Breakerless
Carburettor/Injection	Solex-Pierburg downdraught twin choke
Max power	135bhp (DIN) at 5,200rpm
Max torque	159lb ft at 3,000rpm

Front; rear drive

TRANSMISSION
Type: Three-speed automatic

Gear	Ratio	mph/1,000rpm
3rd	1.00	20.91
2nd	1.47	14.22
1st	2.47	8.46

Final drive gear: Hypoid
Ratio: 3.54

SUSPENSION
Front — location: Independent, double wishbone
 — springs: Coil
 — dampers: Telescopic
 — anti-roll bar: Yes
Rear — location: Live axle, trailing arms, Watts linkage
 — springs: Coil
 — dampers: Telescopic
 — anti-roll bar: Yes

STEERING
Type: Rack and pinion
Power assistance: Optional
Wheel diameter: 14.9in
Turns lock to lock: 2.5

BRAKES
Circuits: Two split front rear
Front: 10.5in dia disc/drum
Rear: 10.6in dia disc/drum
Servo: Vacuum
Handbrake: Centre lever, rear drums

WHEELS
Type: Wolfrace all alloy (option)
Rim width: 6in (5½in steel wheel)
Tyres — make: Dunlop
 — type: SP Sport
 — size: 185HR 14
 — pressures: F24, R24psi (normal driving)

EQUIPMENT
Battery	12v 55Ah
Alternator	55A
Headlamps	220/110W
Reversing lamp	Standard
Electric fuses	16
Screen wipers	2-speed plus intermittent
Screen washer	Electric
Interior heater	Air blending
Air conditioning	Not available
Interior trim	Leather/cloth seats, flock headline
Floor covering	Carpet
Jack	Screw scissor
Jacking points	4, under chassis members
Windscreen	Laminated
Underbody protection	Galvanised chassis — glass fibre body

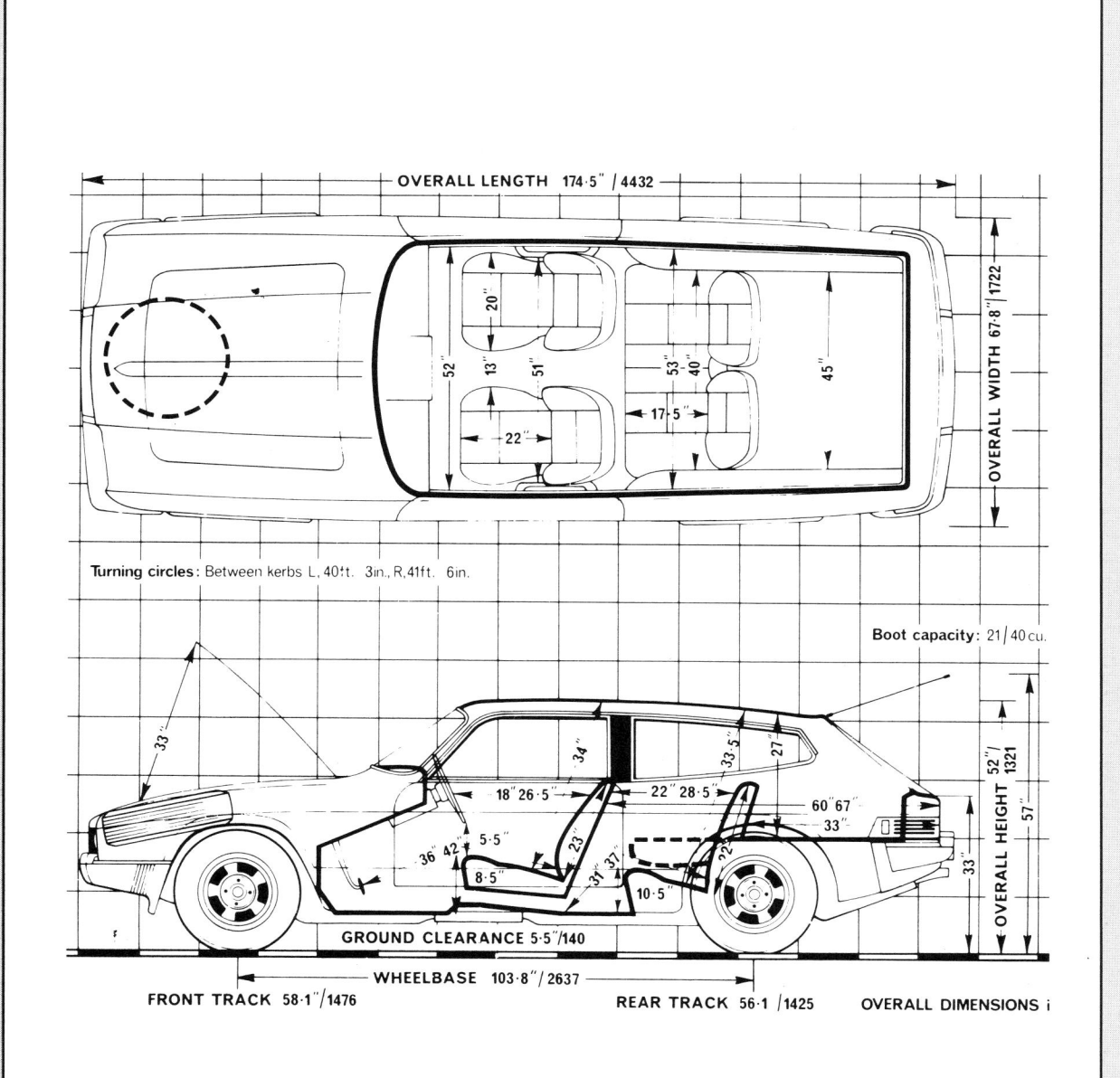

Appendix

RELIANT SCIMITAR SE8b

ENGINE
	Front; rear drive
Head/block	Cast iron
Cylinders	6, in 60deg vee
Main bearing	4
Cooling	Water
Fan	Electric
Bore	93.02mm (3.66in)
Stroke	68.50mm (2.70in)
Capacity	2,792cc (170.38cu in)
Valve gear	Ohv
Camshaft drive	Gears
Compression ratio	9.2-to-1
Ignition	Breakerless
Carburettor	Solex-Pierburg downdraught twin-choke
Max power	135bhp (DIN) at 5,200rpm
Max torque	159lb ft at 3,000rpm

TRANSMISSION
Type: Four-speed manual with overdrive
Clutch: Diaphgragm

Gear	Ratio	mph/1,000rpm
O/D top	0.778	26.88
Top	1.00	20.91
O/D 3rd	1.098	19.04
3rd	1.412	14.81
2nd	1.942	10.77
1st	3.160	6.62

Final drive gear: Hypoid
Ratio: 3.54

SUSPENSION
Front	— location	Independent, wishbone
	— springs	Coil
	— dampers	Telescopic
	— anti-roll bar	Standard
Rear	— location	Live axle, trailing arms, Watt linkage
	— springs	Coil
	— dampers	Telescopic

STEERING
Type	Rack and pinion
Power assistance	Extra (on test car)
Wheel diameter	14.9in
Turns lock to lock	2½

BRAKES
Circuits	Two split front rear
Front	10.5in dia disc
Rear	10.0in dia drum
Servo	Vacuum
Handbrake	Centre lever, rear drums

WHEELS
Type	Wolfrace all alloy (extra)
Rim width	6in (5½in steel wheel)

Tyres — make	Dunlop
— type	SP Sport radial tubeless
— size	185HR × 14
— pressures	F24, R24psi (normal driving)

EQUIPMENT
Battery	12v 55Ah
Alternator	55A
Headlamps	220/110W
Reversing lamp	Standard
Electric fuses	16
Screen wipers	2-speed plus intermittent
Screen washer	Electric
Interior heater	Air blending
Air conditioning	Not available
Interior trim	Leathercloth seats
Floor covering	Carpet
Jack	Screw scissor
Jacking points	4. under chassis members
Windscreen	Laminated
Underbody protection	Galvanised chassis — glass fibre body

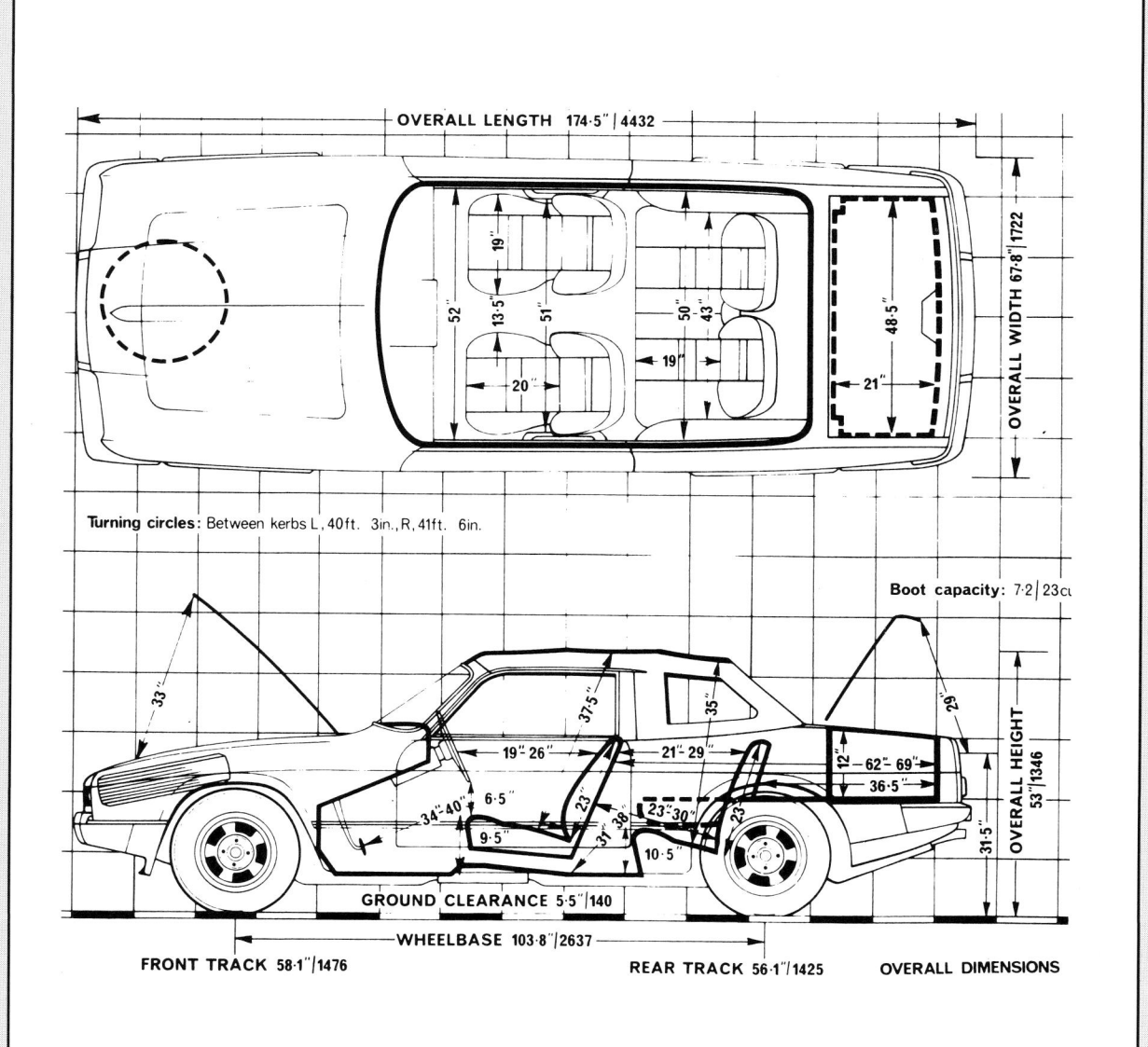

Appendix

RELIANT SCIMITAR SS1

ENGINE 4 cylinder in line, water cooled, four stroke petrol engine. Cast iron cylinder block, aluminium cylinder head with overhead camshaft.

	1300	1600	1800 Ti
Manufacturer	FORD	FORD	NISSAN
Cubic capacity (cc)	1,296	1,596	1,809
Compression ratio	9.5:1	9.5:1	8.0:1
Bore mm/ins.	79.96/3.15	79.96/3.15	83.00/3.27
Stroke mm/ins.	64.52/2.54	79.52/3.13	83.60/3.29
Power DIN kw/PS at	51/69	71/96	99/135
at revs/minute	6,000	6,000	6,000
Torque DIN Nm/lb.ft.	100/74	133/98	191/143
at revs/minute	3,500	4,000	4,000
Ignition	Electronic		
Lubrication	Crankshaft driven gear type pump		

FUEL SYSTEM

Type	Carburettor variable venturi	Carburettor twin venturi	Electronic fuel injection
Choke	manual	automatic	automatic enrichment
Turbo charger	N/A	N/A	water cooled
Fuel pump	mechanical	mechanical	electric
Tank capacity litres/galls.	45.4/10		
Fuel	97 octane (4 star)		

TRANSMISSION

5-speed manual. Cable-operated, single dry plate clutch 8.5in dia.

GEARBOX
Fully synchromesh

	4 speed	mph/1,000rpm	5 speed	mph/1,000rpm	5 speed	mph/1,000rpm
Gear ratios: first	3.58:1	4.68	3.65:1	4.60	3.59:1	4.67
second	2.01:1	8.33	1.97:1	8.52	2.06:1	8.16
third	1.40:1	11.96	1.37:1	12.25	1.36:1	12.34
fourth	1:1	16.75	1:1	16.78	1:1	16.78
fifth	N/A		0.82:1	20.47	0.81:1	20.65
reverse	3.32:1		3.66:1		3.66:1	

Final drive: Hypoid bevel, ratio 3.92.

ROAD WHEELS & TYRES

Wheels	5.00 × 13in. steel	5.00 × 13in. steel	5.50 × 14in alloy
Tyres	175/70R-13-80S steel braced radial ply.	175/70R-13-80S steel braced radial ply.	185/60R-14-82H steel braced radial ply.

SUSPENSION
Front, independent, double wishbones, coil springs, telescopic dampers, anti-roll bar.
 Rear suspension, independent, semi-trailing arms, coil springs, telescopic dampers, anti-roll bar.

STEERING
Rack and pinion. Steering wheel diameter 13½in, 2.9 turns lock to lock.

BRAKES
Dual circuits, H-I split. **Front** 8.9in (226mm) dia discs. **Rear** 8.0in (203mm) dia drums. **Vacuum servo. Handbrake,** centre lever acting on rear drums.

EQUIPMENT
Battery 12V, 60Ah. Alternator 45A. Headlamps 110/120W. Reversing lamp standard. 18 electric fuses. 2-speed, plus intermittent screen wipers. Electric screen washer. Air blending interior heater. Velour cloth seats. Carpet floor covering. Scissor jack; 2 jacking points each side. Laminated windscreen.

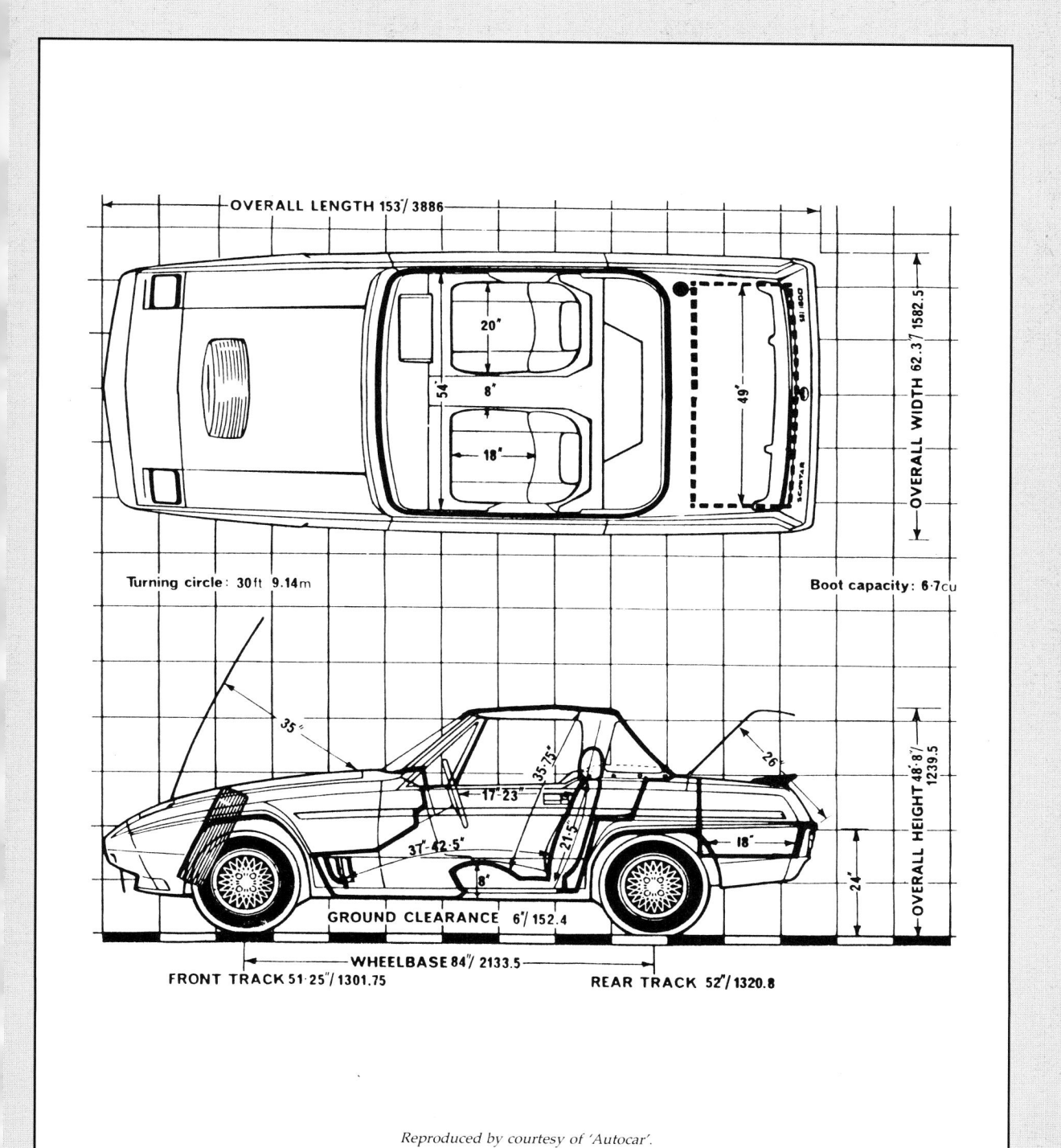

Appendix

Reproduced by courtesy of 'Autocar'.

SABRE & SCIMITAR PERFORMANCE DATA

MODEL	Sabre 4 SE1	Sabre 6 SE2	Sabre 6 Sprint	SE4	SE4a	SE4c	SE5(A)	SE5a(O/D)	SE5a(M)	SE6(A)	SE6a(O/D)	SE6b(A)	SE8b(O/D)	SS1 1600	1800ti
Date	3/62	4/64	12/65	5/65	1/67	9/68	4/70	7/72	2/73	3/76	5/77	1/81	9/80	4/85	9/86
Reg. No.	7946 WD	249 JNX	876 HWD	BUE 442B	ARF 965D	CRE 237F	XRF 978H		NRF 505L	RMC 5L	NOL 644R	1 GTE	EOE 417V	B738 AOA	D966 MOH
Price (£)	1,128	1,075	—	1,292	1,516	1,463	1,998	1,902	2,430	4,446	5,891	10,324	11,360	7,795	9,750
Max speed	90.1	110.5	101	117	121	111	113	119	121	119	118	116	119	108	124
0-30mph (secs)	5.2	3.8	2.1	3.5	3.1	3.9	4.2	3.4	3.0	3.7	3.2	4.1	3.3	3.4	2.8
0-50mph (secs)	11.4	9.2	5.0	8.5	7.2	8.7	8.0	6.8	6.4	7.4	6.9	8.0	7.6	8.1	5.4
0-70mph (secs)	23.5	15.8	8.7	15.1	13.0	16.0	14.3	12.6	11.8	13.4	13.5	14.8	14.2	15.3	9.3
Std-¼ mile (secs)	20.3	18.3	15.2	18.0	17.1	18.5	18.0	16.9	16.9	17.6	17.2	17.8	17.6	18.1	15.5
30-50mph in top (secs)	9.9	7.5	3.8	6.6	6.3	9.2	5.9#	7.2	9.1	5.5#	7.8	5.6#	8.4	12.3	7.9
50-70mph in top (secs)	14.1	9.1	4.5	7.7	6.3	10.7	6.9#	7.8	10.1	6.3#	9.2	7.1#	8.8	14.8	7.1
Touring mpg	34.0	28.0	—	26.0	27.0	28.0	26.5	27.2	27.0	26.4	27.4	26.5	27.3	42.6	28.3
Overall mpg	28.8	20.3	18.6	19.8	22.1	21.7	20.4	20.9	20.8	20.3	21.1	20.5	21.0	32.8	21.8
mph/1,000rpm	19.4	26.1*	20.0	23.9*	24.6*	24.5*	23.5	26.8*	24.8	21.9	28.3*	20.9	26.9*	20.5	20.6
Weight (cwt)	16.3	19.4	18.2	21.5	22.1	21.0	22.7	22.7	21.8	24.8	24.8	24.3	21.6	17.3	17.6

\# Intermediate gear
* Overdrive Top

(By Courtesy of 'Autocar' magazine)

APPENDIX

SCIMITAR GTE/GTC WHEELS

Standard Fibreglass trims
over steel wheels

Top	..	..	SE5	1968-1971
Middle	..	..	SE5a	1972-1976
			SE6/8	1980-1986
Bottom	..	..	SE6/6a	1976-1980

Optional Extra
Alloy wheels

Top	..	..	'GT' SE5	1970-1972
Middle	..	..	Dunlop SE5a/6	1972-1977
Bottom	..	..	Wolfrace SE6/8	1977-1986

Sabre and Scimitar Logos

1961-1964
(SE1 & SE2)

1964-1972
(SE4 & SE5)

1973-1986
(SE5a, SE6a, SE6b, SE8b)

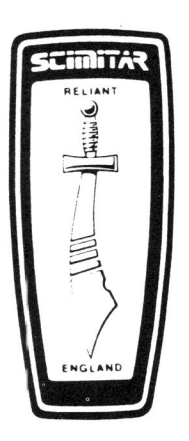

1984-
(SS1 & Ti)

Index

	Page
AEON Rubber	79
ALEXANDER Engeering	26, 30, 44, 45
ALEXANDRE Motors	51
(see also Griffiths, L.)	
ALFA ROMEO	25, 73, 112
ALFORD & ALDER	52
ALPINE	30, 107
ALPINE Rally	52-55
ALVIS 3-litre	63
ANADOL	17-18, 98-99, 102, 186, 191
ANNE, H.R.H. The Princess, (later H.R.H The Princess Royal)	12, 115, 124, 146
ANT	77
ARGYLL Motors	32, 40, 46, 65
ASHLEY Bodyshell	20, 25, 26, 28
ASTLE, Derrick	46-47, 48, 50-53, 62
ASTON, Bob	44, 46-48, 50, 53, 62
ASTON MARTIN	26, 52, 107, 116, 119
AUSTIN...	
7 engine... 4; 750 Motor club... 11; A60 brakes in Sabra... 24; Farina A40 rear lights Sabre 6... 34; 1800... 103; A40 Countryman... 106; Metro... 171.	
AUSTIN HEALEY 3000...	
Compared Sabre 6... 37; test Sabre 4... 45; Astle killed... 53; Alpine rally... 54; compared Scimitar & Sunbeam Tiger... 83; Sprite... 165.	
'AUTOCAR' magazine...	
Test report Sabre 4... 29; Eves advises on Sabre 6... 33; report after modifications... 35-36; figures for hill climb... 63; test report Scimitar... 81; Coupé staff car... 91; test figures SE6a... 140; article by Karen... 189-190.	
AUTOCARS Ltd, Israel...	
Station wagon... 13; co-operative venture... 17; instigate Sabre... 20; engine & gear-box... 26; debut & export to N. America... 27; bumper over-riders... 28; liquidation... 31; co-operation results... 191.	
'AUTOSPORT' magazine	39, 90
B.M.C.	54, 73, 77
B.M.W.	112, 141
B.R.M.	56, 100
BAILEY, Peter	100
BALLAMY, Les	20, 23-26, 35
BARBOUR, John	142
BATMOBILE	185
BAXTER, Raymond	55-56, 62
BEHERMAN, Joseph	142
BENSON & HEDGES Concours 1986	197
BERNADOTTE & BJORNE Design	75
BERTONE	18, 165, 186, 188
BOAM, Peter	148
BODDY, Bill	28, 39, 91
(see also 'Motor Sport')	
BOLSTER, John	39, 90, 91
(see also 'Autosport')	
BOND CARS	9-11, 181-183

	Page
BORG-WARNER	114-138
BORRANI	64
BRISTOL	151
BRITISH GRAND PRIX	86
BRITISH LEYLAND	136, 142, 151, 188, 189
BURTON, Cyril	178
BUSH RADIO	72
CARMEL	13, 17
CATERHAM Super 7	174
CENTRAL SCHOOL OF ARTS & CRAFTS	71
CHATWIN, Ken	48, 50, 55
CHEQUERED FLAG Garage	60
(see also Warner, Graham A.)	
CHETWYND, Tommy	124
CHRISTIE, Michael	45
CIPHER	165-169
CIRCUIT OF IRELAND Rally	51
CITROEN 2CV	12, 23
CLARK, Jim	6
CLARK, Roger	53-55, 62
CLASSIC CAR SHOW, Brighton 1986	197
COMMANDER'S CUP	65
COOPER	74, 100
COOPER, David	50, 62
COOPER, Gerald	46, 47, 53, 62
COTTIER, Bernard	100
COUPÉ DES ALPES	54, 62
COVENTRY HOOD COMPANY	154
CRELLIN, Ron	51, 62
CROSTHWAITE, John	88, 94, 97, 100, 108, 181, 182, 183, 186
DAIMLER...	
SP250 disc brakes... 52; chassis... 71; Ogle SX250... 75; Ogle Daimlers... 78; SE4 components... 80; changes on GTE... 93; comparison with GTE... 112.	
DARLINGTON, Reg	51
DATSUN	136, 140
DAVENPORT, John	51
DAVID OGLE Ltd	74
(see also Ogle Design)	
DEVLIN, Joe	196
DEVLIN, John	196
DIXON, Roy	57, 62
DODD, Ken	32, 40
DOLPHIN	18, 166
DUNFORD & ELLIOTT	3
DUNLOP	117, 139, 171, 186
E. B. Debonair	20
E.R.A	157
EASTON, Peter	43, 44, 62
EDINBURGH, H.R.H. The Duke of	86, 184
EDMONDS, Noel	125
EDWARD, H.R.H. The Prince	160
EQUUS	169
EVES, Edward	33, 35, 80, 81, 91
(see also 'Autocar')	

	Page
FERGUSON	185
FIAT	14, 165, 174, 182
FISHER, Tony	46-48, 50, 51, 53, 62

FORD . . .
  105E Anglia . . . 8; price compared with Rebel . . . 14; Escort price & Kitten . . . 14; parts not for Sabra . . . 23-24; Consul engine for Sabra . . . 26; parts fitted to Sabra . . . 32, 33; Cortina GT . . . 54; Classic Capri features on Scimitar . . . 79; SE4 engine . . . 79; Scimitar gearbox . . . 82; options from Ogle GTS/Zephyr/Zodiac engines . . . 88; Cortina ventilation . . . 89; Zodiac Mk.4 gearbox . . . 90; V8 engine . . . 100; Zephyr/Zodiac design . . . 105; Cortina ventilation . . . 107; Zodiac V6 . . . 108; Cortina door-handle . . . 117; Granada . . . 119; gearboxes . . . 120; Capri . . . 125, 136; V6 engine . . . 136; C3 gearboxes . . . 138; Capri test figures . . . 140; new V6 engines . . . 142, 143; Capri . . . 148; V6 engines . . . 157; units for SS1 . . . 168; Sierra . . . 170; Escort . . . 171; V8 engine . . . 185; Transits & D100 . . . 191; RS200 Group B rally cars . . . 191.

FOX	18, 166
GARRETT	178
GENERAL MOTORS	169
GINETTA	5
GIRLING	120, 136, 138, 139
GOAD, David	45
GOOD, Tony	142
GRIFFITHS, Alex	51, 57, 58, 62
GRIFFITHS, Leslie	51, 54, 62
GULBENKIAN, Nubar	85
HAMILTON, Robin	148
HARRIS MANN	182
HEALEY, Donald	142
HEALEY, Keith	23
HERON, Roger	195
HILLMAN	8, 9, 11, 14, 107
HODGE GROUP	5, 110, 142
HODGE, Lady	110
HODGE, Sir Julian	5
HODGKINSON BENNIS	5
HONDA AERODECK	190
HOPKIRK, Paddy	54
HOPWOOD, John	46, 47, 62
HUGHES, Michael	48, 62
HUMBER (Sceptre)	113
HYUNDAI CAR COMPANY	186
ISSIGONIS, Alec	109
JACKSON, Peter	100
JAGUAR	56, 63, 119, 141, 157
JENSEN HEALEY	116
JENSEN Interceptor	186

	Page
KAREN, Tom	10, 72, 75, 97, 99, 100, 110, 126, 132, 133, 152, 181, 189-190
KENNING GROUP	115
KING, John	46, 62
KITTEN	14, 15, 165, 166
LAMBORGHINI Espada	97
LANCIA	140, 141, 151
LAYCOCK	82, 120
LE MANS	43, 63
LEBAN, Ted	185
LESTON, Les	26
LOBB, Alex	55, 62
LOCKHEED	120, 138
LOEWY, Raymond	72
LORD, Leonard	109

LOTUS . . .
  Fibreglass . . . 5; ZF S4-12 . . . 26; returned ZF boxes . . . 31; SE4's bought to transplant ZF boxes . . . 82; Crosthwaite . . . 100; Elan . . . 125; dealers . . . 137; Elan . . . 165; bonnet . . . 171; Espirit . . . 182.

LUCAS	107
LYNX	189

MGA, MGB, MGC etc . . .
  Compared Sabre 4 . . . 30; Sabre 6 . . . 37; GT-3-litre, MGC GT, SE4c & TR5 . . . 92; MGB rear brake parts . . . 138; axed . . . 151; Midget, MGB . . . 165.

McCARTHY, Mike	157
McCAULEY, John	148
MacMILLEN, Ernest	57, 62
MAKINEN, Timo	53, 54
MARCOS	5
MARSH, Tony	64
MARSLAND, Robert	64
MAYS, Raymond	52
MEADOWS, Frisky	25
MERCEDES	137, 141, 151, 158, 159
MICHELOTTI	77, 165, 168, 169, 182
MICROCELL	30
MIDDLEBRIDGE Engineering	148, 190
MIDLAND HILL CLIMB CHAMPIONSHIP 1986	197
MINI 1000	12, 14, 109
MINTEX	44, 48
MOBIL Economy Run	16
MONKHOUSE, Bob	10
MONTAGUE, Lord	86

MONTE CARLO RALLY . . .
  1963 . . . 48, 50, 51; 1964 . . . 58, 60, 61

MORGAN	151, 174
MORLEY, Don	54
MORRIS, Martin	157
MOSS, Stirling	90

'MOTOR' magazine . . .
  Test report Sabre 4 . . . 29-30; test report Sabre 6 . . . 36; test summary GTE . . . 112

INDEX

MOTOR SHOW . . .
    1961 Debut Sabre 4 sports . . . 28; 1962 Sabre 6 . . . 34; Ogle Design . . . 71; Ogle SX250 . . . 75; 1964 launch of Scimitar . . . 80; Ogle GTS . . . 85; 1967 . . . 97; 1968 . . . 109; 1969 . . . 113 & 114; 1971 . . . 116; 1973 . . . 122; 1975 . . . 136; 1984 . . . 171; Geneva 1977 . . . 186

'MOTOR SPORT' magazine . . .
    Editorial comment Kitten . . . 16; Sabre . . . 28, 39; Scimitar . . . 91

'MOTORING NEWS' 46, 51
MOTTRAM, Reg 94
MUNRO, Bob 43
MURPHY RADIO 71

NASH, J. F. 142
NASH SECURITIES 142
NERUS 45
NEW YORK MOTOR SHOW 1961 27
NIMROD ASTON MARTIN racing team 148
NISSAN SILVIA 1800 Turbo 176
NIXON, David 125

OGIER, John 75
OGLE, David 71-75
OGLE DESIGN . . .
    Bond Bug . . . 9; new body for Regal . . . 11; Rebel body . . . 14; Anadol (FW5) . . . 17; early exhibits & history . . . 71-75; SX250 . . . 71; Ogle 1.5 . . . 73; Ogle Mini (SX1000) . . . 74; Fletcher GT . . . 75; Ogle SX250 . . . 75-77; body fitted to Sabra chassis . . . 78-80; Ogle GTS . . . 84-86; SE4a . . . 90; GTE . . . 97-99; Ogle GTE . . . 110; GTS . . . 115; SE6 . . . 132, 134; convertible . . . 151, 152, 154; prototype . . . 181; GTS . . . 184; Ogle Daimler . . . 185

'OLD MOTOR' magazine 157
OLSEN, Carl 75
OSMOND, Ed 165, 169, 188
OTOSAN Company (Istanbul) 17, 188

PAGE, David 17, 23-25, 63, 79, 81, 102
PARK, Dave 100
PARKES, Bobby 53, 58, 62, 100
PARKES, Lai 48, 50, 62, 100
PATRICK MOTOR GROUP 146
PECK, Derek 186, 188
PEPALL, Eddie 33, 34, 45
PERSPEX 53, 79
PININFARINA 77
PIRELLI 29, 35
POMEROY TROPHY 195
PORSCHE (928) 110, 137, 171, 189
PRESS OPERATIONS 5

229

R.A.C. Rally . . .
    1962 . . . 44-47; 1963 . . . 57
R.S.S.O.C. 195-198
RACING CAR SHOW, 1963 75
RALEIGH 3
RAY, Jimmy 46-48, 50, 53-55, 62
REBEL 14, 77, 80
REGAL 4, 8, 9, 50, 51
REGENT 4
RENAULT 106, 166, 168
RESTALL 107
REW, Robin 195
RIALTO 12
RICHARDS, Robin 55, 62
RILEY 1.5 73
RILEY, Peter 45, 46
ROBERTS, Peter 46, 48, 53, 58, 62
ROBIN 11, 12, 16, 186
ROLT, Tony 185
ROUTLEDGE, Martin 48, 50
ROVER 63, 97, 136, 166, 188
ROWLEY, Roger 197
RUSLING, Arthur 43-46, 48, 51-52, 53-58, 62, 63-65

SABRA . . .
    Autocars of Israel . . . 20; project development . . . 23-26; debut New York Motor Show 1961 . . . 27; exported N. America . . . 27; not for UK . . . 71; first 4-wheel convertible . . . 151, 191

SABRE . . .
    Sabra to Sabre 4 . . . 28; test reports . . . 29, 30; Sabre 4 comparison chart . . . 30; returned ZF gearboxes . . . 31; advertising . . . 32; poor sales . . . 32; 6 cylinder Ford engine . . . 32; Sabre 6 development . . . 33, 34; Sabre 6 at 1962 Motor Show . . . 34; Sabre 4 body modifications . . . 35; Sabre 6 front suspension modifications . . . 35; comparison chart . . . 37; show business personalities . . . 40; works Sabre 4 last outing . . . 51; Sabre 6 model for future . . . 51; Rally achievements . . . 62; private race entries . . . 65; Sabre 6 aimed at GT market . . . 65; racing Sabre 6 . . . 184

SALISBURY 33, 52, 60, 119, 136
SANDFORD, Cecil 50, 62
SCIMITAR . . .
    GT(SE4) launched . . . 80; journalists' comments . . . 80, 81; comparison Healey 3000 & Sunbeam Tiger . . . 83; basis of Ogle GTS . . . 84; suspension improvements . . . 88; SE4a . . . 89; test reports . . . 90-91; comparison GT3-litre, MGC GT, 2.5 SE4c & TR5 . . . 92; Coupé ceases production . . . 94; GTE . . . 97-128; Coupé . . . 100, 102, 180, 110, 114; SE5a . . . 116; 120, 121; SE6 . . . 131-138; SE6a . . . 138-142; SE6b . . . 143-145; Convertible . . . 144; last GTE . . . 146; GTC . . . 151-161; SS1 . . . 173; 1800Ti . . . 176-178; SS1 . . . 182; Coupé . . . 184; SE6 . . . 185; FW11 . . . 186; prototypes . . . 181-191

	Page
SCOTT, Tom	44, 100, 122
SENIOR, Arthur	55, 62
750 MOTOR Club	11
SHENSTON	6
SHUBINSKY, Mr	20
SKEFFINGTON, David	48, 62
'SLICE'	198
SMITHS FORGINGS	5
SNOWDON, Lord	85
SPA-SOFIA-LIEGE	55-56
SPENCER, Ritchie	18, 142, 144, 151, 160, 165, 168, 169, 175, 178, 188
SPIERS, John	62
STANDARD Vanguard	24, 77
STEERING WHEEL GARAGE	65
(see also WARNER, Graham P.)	
STEVENS, Tony	165, 167, 168, 169
SUNBEAM TIGER	83, 119
SUNDYM	85
SUNRISE AUTO INDUSTRIES (SAIL)	18
SUSSITA	13, 17, 20
SWINGER, Peter	65

TARBUCK, Jimmy	10
THATCHER, Mrs	124
THOMPSON, Colin	23, 33
THOMPSON, 'Tommo'	4
THORPE, Jevon	171
TIPLER, Roger	195
TOYOTA (MR2)	177
TRAFFORD, Les	197
TRANA, Tom	53
TRIPLEX	84-86, 97
TRIUMPH... Vitesse running gear... 9; Herald & Spitfire bonnet & front wing... 26; GT6 profile... 34; double wishbones & Herald steering rack... 35; TR4 cf. Sabre 6... 37; TR4 wishbone IFS... 52; Spitfire steering rack... 52; 2000 headlamp... 79; Scimitar GT 3-litre cf. MGC GT, SE4c & TR5... 92; TR6 front suspension... 93; 1300... 118; Stag... 125; Mayflower... 128; interior design SE6... 134; TR6, TR7, Spitfire & Stag... 151; Stag... 152, 154, 158; TR6, TR7, Spitfire... 165; TR7... 171, 182;	
TULIP INTERNATIONA RALLY... 1962... 43-44; 1963... 53	
TURNBULL, George	186
TURNER, Stuart	62
TVR	5, 30, 116
TWELL, Barry	50

V.S.C.C.	195
VALLER, Roger	28, 196
John	28, 196
VAUXHALL Victor	107
Equus	169
'VERGLAS'	51
(see also DAVENPORT, John)	
VOLVO	123, 125, 141

WARNER, Graham A.	60-62
WARNER, Graham P.	57, 60, 62, 65
WATTS, Mike	65
WAYNE, Reg	32
WEBASTO	121
WEBB, Ossy	185
WEBER	52, 55, 56
WIGGIN, Ray	5, 10, 13, 14, 17, 18, 23, 28, 31, 32, 33, 40, 43, 46, 52, 58, 65, 71, 77, 78, 81, 97, 99, 100, 106, 109, 126, 131, 142, 186, 188, 191
WILKINSON, 'Wilkie'	56
WILLIAMS, Danny	40
WILLIAMS, Tom Lawrence	3, 5, 14, 23, 71
WILLS, Barrie	186, 188
WILMOTT, Jerry	191
WILSON-SPRATT, Doug	55, 62
WISDOM, Norman	40
WOLFRACE	139, 159
WOOD, Ken	17, 23, 25, 78-80, 100, 131, 153, 182
WOOD-JEFFRIES	119

| ZF S4-12 | 26, 28, 31, 44, 65, 82 |

The author with his Sabre 6 (92 FRP) which gave him tremendous fun and some success while racing it during 1978-1984.

DON PITHER was born in 1939, the younger son of a Gloucestershire farmer. He was educated at the Crypt School, Gloucester, before studying for a Chemistry degree at Worcester College, Oxford. After a short period with Shell Chemical Co. in Manchester and London he forsook his scientific career for one in farming on the death of his father in 1965. During this phase he formed an animal feed milling company, Mixfeed Ltd in 1970, which he sold in 1982 to establish his present company Scimpart Ltd, purveying Scimitar spares and accessories. His love of cars was stimulated by the arrival of his father's first new car, an Austin A40 Somerset in 1952, leading to the purchase of his first car, an Austin 7 after returning from National Service in Cyprus during 1957-59. It was in Cyprus that Don Pither first had his taste of rallying in an MG Magnette and he was able to continue this interest while at Oxford in a Mini van, actually winning one small event with it.

After owning a succession of cars including Alfa Romeo Giulietta Sprint, Triumph 2000 and BMW 2002 he acquired a long admired Scimitar GTE in 1976 which he still possesses and is featured on the front cover of this book. Married for the second time in 1983 he now has two sons and a daughter ranging from 18 years to 18 months.

This is his first book, but he has contributed a variety of motoring articles to 'Old Motor', 'Sporting Cars', 'Classic & Sportscar' and 'Sports Car Monthly' during the past five years.